ADVANCED MOTORING

ADVANCED MOTORING

Expert advice and information
on advanced motoring techniques
compiled by the
Institute of Advanced Motorists

Third Edition

Institute of Advanced Motorists

Published in association with the
Institute of Advanced Motorists

First published in 1967 by Queen Anne Press,
3rd Floor, Greater London House, Hampstead Road,
London NW1 7QX.

Reprinted 1967
Revised edition 1969
Reprinted 1969, 1971, 1972, 1973, 1975
New edition 1976
Reprinted 1977, 1978
Revised and updated 1982
Reprinted 1985, 1986, 1987

This edition first published in 1989 by
Kogan Page Ltd,
120 Pentonville Road, London N1 9JN
in association with the Institute of Advanced Motorists,
IAM House, 359/365 Chiswick High Road, London W4 4HS.

Reprinted 1990

Printed and bound in Great Britain by Richard Clay Ltd

British Library Cataloguing in Publication Data
Advanced motoring.—3rd ed.
  1. Cars. Driving. Manuals
  I. Institute of Advanced Motorists
  629.28'32

ISBN 1-85091-913-5

Contents

FOREWORD

It may be that, by international standards, British road users are a relatively safe group of people and our accident rate is among the lowest in Europe; all this despite the fact that the weight of traffic is very heavy indeed. Even so, our safety performance on the roads is not exactly a matter for self-congratulation. The annual toll in terms of death and injury – not to mention the vast expense of it all – is still depressingly high.

What is happening to cut this toll? First, the authorities regularly modify the rules and regulations governing road users in an effort to reduce the accident rate. And secondly, private groups, from accident prevention organisations to vehicle manufacturers, are continually striving to reduce the chances of an accident occurring in the first place, and to minimise its effects when the seemingly inevitable does occur. But this is not really enough, for almost no one is tackling the problem from the point of view of the driver.

This is where the Institute of Advanced Motorists comes in. It is our belief that the single most effective way open to any of us to reduce accidents is to press for a better standard of driving. The Institute was founded, with this aim in view, in 1956 at the suggestion of the (then) Minister of Transport. As a voluntary non-profit-earning charity, the Institute's primary purpose is to evaluate the driving standards of motorists who present themselves for the advanced test.

Passing or failing the test is not necessarily the main object: the evaluation, carried out by one of the Institute's examiners (all of whom hold a Class One Police driving certificate), is what counts. From this assessment candidates can learn what is right in their driving and, much more important, what they should do to improve from a safety point of view. But even taking the advanced test implies a responsible attitude to good driving.

The Institute's method of driving, based on practices tried and tested by the police, is a clearly defined though not inflexible one. This method is set out in the pages of this book. Simply reading *Advanced Motoring* will, I believe, make you a better driver. But if you can put into practice on the road all that you can read here, you will become a thoroughly responsible motorist and a very safe driver indeed.

Major General E. H. G. Lonsdale, CB, MBE, MA, FCIT
Vice-President,
Institute of Advanced Motorists
Stogursey, Somerset

INTRODUCTION – THE NEED FOR ADVANCED DRIVING

Around 310,000 people, equivalent to the population of Coventry, are killed or injured every year on Britain's roads. Over 5000 die, 65,000 are seriously injured and another 240,000 are less badly hurt. Someone is injured every 101 seconds and a death occurs every 102 minutes. By the time you have read this page, someone – driver, passenger, cyclist, motorcyclist or pedestrian – will have been hurt in a road accident. Before long, there will be another death.

A high proportion of those killed and injured are children and young people. In some groups – among young men, for example – road accidents are the single most likely cause of death, outweighing all kinds of disease. The death toll is the equivalent of a major air disaster occurring every week in Britain. Even though the number of road casualties has been dropping gradually over the past 25 years, and despite the fact that many European countries have a far grimmer record, we have a long way to go.

Improve your safety record

Since you have chosen to read this book, we would think that you have a responsible attitude to road safety. Many of us live in a secure bubble which tells us that 'it will never happen to me', but we must face the fact that *everyone* is vulnerable. There is a good chance that you, or someone close to you, will be involved in a road accident. Despite the fact that cars are becoming safer, better roads are being built and road safety is receiving greater emphasis in our classrooms and on our television screens, we all have a duty to become more aware of the dangers of driving. Each one of us can act immediately and have a more significant effect on road safety than any of these improvements, because human error is responsible for the majority of road accidents. We can improve our driving, and the purpose of this book is to guide you in the technique of being a better driver.

Advanced Motoring has been compiled by the Institute of Advanced Motorists to take drivers who have already passed from the O level of the Government driving test on to the A level standard of advanced driving. The guidance in this book is based on the driving methods used by the Institute's examiners, who are all former Class One police drivers. It will not teach you to be a faster driver, or to make quicker progress in traffic queues, for such tricks have no place in road safety. But it does contain the wisdom accumulated over years of driving safely and with courtesy.

More statistics prove the value of advanced driving techniques. Nearly 300,000 drivers have taken the advanced driving test since the Institute was founded in 1956. Around 70 per cent have passed, and a survey by the Government's Transport and Road Research Laboratory (TRRL) has shown that those who are successful have, on average, a 25 per cent lower accident rate than those who fail, and a 50 to 70 per cent better record than the general motoring public. Institute members, adds the TRRL survey, not only have fewer accidents, but those in which they are involved tend to be less serious. Some insurers recognise these facts by offering favourable terms to those who have been successful in the advanced driving test. This all proves that the Minister of Transport in 1956 was right to press for an organisation to improve driving standards through an advanced driving test.

After the Government driving test

The driver who proudly throws away his L-plates is only *beginning* the process of learning how to drive. His apprenticeship is complete, leaving him ready to develop his skills, and learn new ones, so that he can reach the standard of master craftsman. Only then can he regard himself as a safe and responsible motorist, but never must he become complacent because the skills can be refined still further throughout his driving life. This manual aims to provide all the information necessary for you to make sure that your best workmanship always goes into the art of driving safely.

Much of what follows concentrates on driving technique, but advice about how to make sure that your car is fit for the road is also included. Do remember that *Advanced Motoring* is a practical guide to driving, not a legal textbook. It does not aim to provide a detailed guide to motoring rules and regulations. The *Highway Code* is the basis for learning about motoring; *Advanced Motoring* completes your driving course.

2

PLANNING

A systematic and planned approach to every action you take behind the wheel is the basis of advanced driving. There is a procedure for all circumstances, but it must not be inflexible because you need to continually adapt to changing situations. If you are mindful of the procedure, you can be reasonably satisfied that you are equipped to cope with any incidents which occur on the road near you; you need never be caught out by an emergency nor panicked into making a wrong decision. You will drive with a keen awareness of active road safety, anticipating the possible moves of other road users and avoiding situations which could end in an accident.

Sticking to a planned system of driving reduces the chances of surprising other road users. Frequently drivers involved in accidents protest that they are blameless because someone else unexpectedly braked, accelerated, pulled out or turned right. A methodical, planned approach by the errant party would have avoided a dangerous situation, but better anticipation and less trust in the ability of others would have enabled the aggrieved driver also to prevent an accident. Throughout this book, the system of *driving with anticipation* is described in detail; there is a driving plan to be applied to almost any situation.

Can My Safety Be Given Away?

An example can illustrate the point. When turning, approaching a junction or driving round a hazard such as a parked car or roadworks, follow this sequence: Course, Mirror, Signal, Brake, Gear, Acceleration. Commit it to memory with a mnemonic to remind you of the six initials: Can My Safety Be Given Away? This is how the procedure works on the road:

- *Course*: Mentally select the correct course you intend to take.
- *Mirror*: Check your mirror before changing course or altering speed.
- *Signal*: Signal (if necessary) clearly and in good time to confirm your intention to change course. Remember that clear signals assist all road users, including pedestrians.
- *Brake*: Apply the brakes when the car is travelling on a straight path to ensure correct road speed for a lower gear selection if required for maximum car control.
- *Gear*: Select the gear required according to the severity of the hazard, in order to arrive at the hazard travelling at the correct speed, with the correct gear engaged and on the right part of the road.
- *Acceleration*: Accelerate gently at first, according to road and traffic conditions, and apply more progressive acceleration if it is safe to proceed.

Commentary driving

While you are getting used to this system, try 'commentary driving' to show yourself how well you are assessing the conditions around you. Even when you feel that your anticipation is good, this is a useful exercise to keep a running check on your standard. Simply commentate to yourself, describing what you are doing and thinking as you drive along. You may feel uncomfortable at first, but you will realise its value when you become accustomed to it. Do not worry about what other people may think when they see you talking to yourself! A typical commentary might sound like this:

> Turning into School Lane, must be a reason for the name – accelerating away in second gear, moving up to third – make sure the indicator has cancelled – keep an eye on speed, the limit is 30mph – sign ahead indicates limit will be 40mph, but a school warning follows it – it's mid-afternoon and children might be about – slow down a little even though the limit allows more, stay in third – there's a pair of feet visible behind that parked van, could be a child waiting to

cross or dash out – sound a warning on the horn and prepare to move well out into the road, keeping an eye on that concealed entrance on the right – check mirror first – now signal – move out – we're past the school buildings, now in 40mph limit – speed increases, into fourth – check the mirror – there's a parked car ahead, right on the approach to that sharp bend – someone is in the driving seat so it could move off – yes, a puff of smoke from the exhaust so he has started the engine – good idea to hang back a little, even though another car is sitting far too close behind – just as well I did – there he goes, pulling out without even a glance in his mirror, let alone a signal – following him through the bend, keeping a little to the right so I can get maximum vision through this left-hander.

At first you will almost certainly be amazed how much of this sort of detailed planning and observation you have neglected in the past. With a little practice, however, you should surprise yourself with how much more observant you become. Assessing all the information and potential hazards around you long before you reach them is one of the fundamentals of advanced driving.

A five-minute session of commentary driving used to form part of the advanced test, but it has now been omitted because the Institute recognises that those inexperienced in it cannot always do themselves justice. Although some excellent drivers find it difficult to articulate their thoughts while concentrating on the task in hand, it is still worth practising. Advanced motorists regard commentary driving as very valuable, so it remains a voluntary part of the test which candidates can include if they wish to reinforce the examiner's impression of their powers of observation.

Summary

- *Anticipate* all road and traffic conditions ahead of you.
- Always apply a planned *procedure* to your driving.
- Practise *commentary driving* so that you regularly monitor your powers of observation and anticipation.

SAFETY AT THE WHEEL

Two aspects of safety at the wheel are covered in this chapter. First, it is important to adopt the right driving position and to make sure that the seat is positioned correctly in relation to steering wheel and pedals. Second, a car's safety features – items like mirrors, safety belts and head restraints – need to be used properly.

Driving position

One of the basic requirements of safe driving is to sit at the wheel properly. If your driving position is wrong, you reduce the degree of control you have over your vehicle and driving becomes unnecessarily tiring. It will also reveal to a trained observer your inadequacies as a driver. Many drivers sit either too close to or too far from the wheel, with the former the more common mistake. Others are simply too casual in their approach.

Sitting too close to the wheel usually suggests that a driver lacks confidence in his ability to handle the car, although poor eyesight is another reason. A driver may not be aware of any defect in his eyesight because deterioration generally creeps up gradually, and he compensates for it unconsciously by placing himself as close as possible to the windscreen. Regardless of the reason, sitting too close to the wheel is tiring and restricts a driver's control of the steering.

On the other hand, you can make the mistake of being too relaxed. It may feel comfortable to hold the steering wheel low down only with the right hand, with elbow resting on the door-pull or window-sill, but control in an emergency is severely impaired. One-handed steering –

perhaps with the hand casually holding a spoke of the wheel – points to over-confidence, almost to the point of boredom, or laziness. The driver of a car with power steering needs to be especially aware of developing lazy habits. Just because it is possible to steer with the little finger doesn't mean that it is safe to do so; again, it is impossible, with such minimal control, to deal efficiently with a sudden avoidance manoeuvre, and your concentration can lapse if you become too relaxed.

The 'boy racer' who seeks to emulate his racing driver heroes by reclining in the cockpit of his car, arms outstretched to a tiny steering wheel, is also at fault. A would-be racer who thinks a laid back position is suitable for his modest saloon can learn, to his cost, that procedures suitable for a racing circuit are to be avoided on the road.

A racing driver's straight-arm position is dictated by lack of space in a narrow cockpit, by sensitive steering which requires just a flick of the wrists to change direction, by his small steering wheel and by the aerodynamic logic of lying well back in a low-slung car. This style of driving is not only irrelevant on the road, but also reduces the driver's control and is as tiring as sitting hunched over the wheel.

So, with the wrong driving positions dealt with, we can turn our attention to the right one. It should allow your hands to sit naturally at either a 'ten-to-two' or 'quarter-to-three' position on the steering wheel while keeping your arms bent at the elbow at an angle of between 90 and 120 degrees. Your legs need to be positioned comfortably in relation to the pedals: they should not be splayed out either side of the steering wheel, nor should you sit so far away that you have to stretch to press the clutch pedal to the floor.

Although people come in all sorts of shapes, sizes and proportions, most cars these days have enough seat travel and backrest rake adjustment to enable the majority of drivers to find a good position. If you are unusually tall or short, it goes without saying that you should check whether you can find a comfortable driving position before choosing which car to buy. Once your driving position is right, you will find that the car becomes easier, less wearing and more pleasurable to drive, all of which contribute to safety at the wheel.

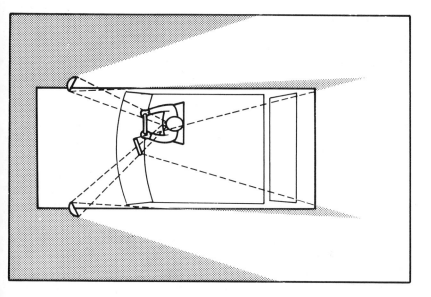

This diagram shows the field of rearward view provided by a good set of mirrors. Always check that they are correctly adjusted in relation to your position at the wheel, or those tantalising blind spots near the rear wings might enlarge sufficiently to hide a cyclist or other hazard. Incidentally, door mirrors are becoming more and more common and have certain advantages over the wing mirrors illustrated here.

Mirrors

As your link with all the outside world which lies behind your peripheral vision, mirrors are vitally important. A good interior mirror giving a broad field of vision, preferably right up to the blind spots formed by the rear quarter panels between the rear screen and rear side windows, is essential so that you have a clear view of what is happening behind. Car design has progressed sufficiently for most modern cars to have good interior mirrors, but if your vehicle has an inadequate mirror it would be wise to buy, from an accessory shop, a larger mirror which can be attached to the front of the standard one. Although convex glass provides a wider field of vision, a larger area of plain glass is preferable because a distorted image gives a false impression of distance.

If the interior mirror vibrates, as many do, find some means of bracing it gently against the windscreen or roof panel; the distance of a fuzzy image of a car is very difficult to judge. Most modern cars are also equipped with a handy anti-dazzle adjustment which is useful in eliminating the distraction caused at night by a following vehicle on main beam. It is worth remembering, though, that using this facility can also alter your perception of distance (it can make headlights seem further away at a glance), so make sure that you adjust the mirror back to its normal position when the dazzling lights have gone.

In recent years it has become almost universal practice for manufacturers to fit exterior mirrors at the front of the doors, rather than in their traditional position out on the car's wings. While a few cars demand rather too much head movement and refocusing of the eyes, properly adjusted door mirrors generally complete the view which is not visible in the interior mirror, and are particularly valuable on dual carriageways and motorways. Cars of more basic specification may have only one mirror on the driver's side, or in a few cases no exterior mirror at all, so it is worth considering fitting one of the many types available on the market.

Since door mirrors are larger than the old-fashioned wing mirrors, they are more vulnerable to being knocked out of adjustment by pedestrians, or even by a passing car in a narrow street. Although a driver can adjust the door mirror by reaching out of the window while on the move, or by twiddling the interior lever or electric control knob, it is good practice always to check the mirrors before driving off. It is stupid to try to alter the position of a near-side mirror by leaning over to manipulate the interior lever while driving along.

Safety belts

The first thing to be said about safety belts is that their use by front seat occupants is compulsory. Apart from special cases exempt from this law (individuals excused on medical grounds or drivers engaged in local deliveries in a vehicle designed for this purpose), the only occasion when you are legally allowed to unfasten your safety belt while driving is when carrying out a manoeuvre which includes reversing.

The majority of new cars are fitted with inertia-reel belts, but many older cars have static belts. Inertia-reel belts remain slack in normal driving so that the user is free to lean forward, perhaps to reach awkwardly placed controls, but they lock when the inertia of the car changes with a sudden application of the brakes. Although people used to be sceptical about their operation, they have proved virtually fail-safe as long as the self-locking device remains in perfect working order. Make sure, though, that nothing on the floor, such as an umbrella, can slide across and jam the reel if it is exposed. It is wise every now and then to check that the webbing has not frayed against the edge of the reel. If your car has static belts, wear them tightly so that they can serve their purpose in the event of an accident. If you carry several different front-seat passengers, do not allow them to neglect to tighten the belt just because it seems difficult.

All new cars must now be fitted with rear seat belts, which usually take the form of proper three-point harnesses for two passengers and a lap strap for an occasional third passenger in the middle. Their use is not yet compulsory but is certainly advisable: an unrestrained rear passenger becomes a dangerous moving object in the event of an accident.

Young children, usually those under 10, are too small to wear adult belts properly, and should be protected by a child safety seat approved by the British Standards Institution. There are many varieties on the market, including clever two-stage ones suitable from birth to four years of age. Most seats come with a miniature version of an adult four-point harness which no child can wriggle out of.

Other safety equipment

Head restraints, often designed as an integral part of the seat, help to prevent serious whiplash injuries to the upper vertebrae caused by the head snapping back if a vehicle crashes into the back of your car. If a head restraint is of suitable design it can also serve as a head rest for a weary passenger; as a driver, however, you should not be tempted to rest your head if you are tired – it is far safer to take a break from the wheel.

Basic safety equipment in your car should include a first aid kit and a fire extinguisher, which should be securely attached to the car, perhaps under a front seat. Choose a good brand with an adequate capacity of the BCF chemical capable of dealing with both petrol and electrical fires.

Regular checks should be carried out on tyre pressure and condition, lights, brakes, steering, windscreen wipers and washers, as well as other safety-related items listed in your car's instruction manual.

Before leaving the subject of safety at the wheel, a few words are necessary about the use of car telephones. Most of us have seen for ourselves examples of the potential danger which exists when a driver holds a car telephone handset while his vehicle is moving. He may vary his speed unnecessarily, react late to hazards or drift from side to side in the road; all in all, as well as being illegal this is a recipe for disaster. The *Highway Code* states the rules very clearly: do not use a hand-held microphone or telephone handset while your car is moving, except in an emergency. If you do wish to have a telephone fitted to your car, insist on a hands-free installation; even then, use the telephone only when it would not distract your attention from the road. Even with a hands-free telephone, it is best to park the car safely before answering or making a call. While all this suggests that telephones and cars should not go together, there is one very valuable benefit in being able to make calls from your car. If congestion makes you late for an important appointment, you can remove any stress and worry, which can affect your standard of driving, by making a call to explain your delay.

Summary

- Adopt the correct *driving position*, with hands on the steering wheel at 'ten-to-two' or 'quarter-to-three'. Position the seat to give a comfortable posture; do not sit hunched over the wheel or too far from it.

- Keep interior and exterior *mirrors* properly adjusted to give a complete field of vision.
- Always wear a *safety belt*, even when travelling in the back of a car with rear belts fitted. Static belts should be worn tightly.

4

A STATE OF MIND

Car ownership is a right which can be enjoyed by every adult of sound body and mind, but there must be some degree of control over the use of cars in the interests of safety and traffic flow. The regulations affecting our use – speed limits, parking restrictions, vehicle condition requirements – are essential to prevent the bedlam which might otherwise break out with 22 million licensed vehicles on the roads. While owning a car is a right, the licence to drive it is a privilege which must be earned and respected. You must first acquire enough skill and responsibility at the wheel to pass the Government driving test, which is less rigorous than in many other countries, and your subsequent entitlement to a licence depends upon maintaining a minimum standard of safe and law-abiding driving. Should you fall below standard, you can be kept off the road through disqualification.

Be positive

The frame of mind with which you approach your driving is important. Apprehension and aggression can be equally dangerous. The nervous driver who hangs back and fails to make a decision when faced with a hazard can be just as likely to cause an accident as the hooligan who drives without care and consideration for other road users, or for himself.

Enjoy your motoring – the techniques of advanced driving will help you derive more pleasure from travelling by car – but be careful to keep your pleasure under control. Do not allow your enjoyment of driving early on a bright spring morning, when there is little traffic about, to cause your speed to creep up unnoticed.

Be courteous

Take pride in being a tolerant and courteous driver at all times. No matter how angry another driver's aggression may make you, never retaliate: all this does is to increase danger and stress. Your own manner and driving standard should never be affected by the stupidity of others on the road, and may act as an example. But do not be over-zealous in setting an example to others: we have all seen the foolish technique of a few drivers in showing their objection to a centre lane hog on a motorway by cutting sharply across his bows after overtaking.

Be considerate

Some drivers, unintentionally or deliberately, accelerate when being overtaken, which is obviously a dangerous practice. Some people perhaps have a natural instinct to stay in front and may press the accelerator a fraction harder, perhaps without realising it. This means that an overtaking driver is exposed on the wrong side of the road for longer than necessary; he may be forced to cut in sharply after he has passed, or change his mind, brake hard and pull in behind. You must always be careful never to endanger another road-user.

Be controlled

While it is simple enough to insist that motorists retain their dignity and courtesy at all times, there are occasions when the most self-controlled driver is affected by outside stresses. Although it is difficult to assess what degree of emotional stress makes a driver a danger on the road, everyone at some time would be better off by understanding the symptoms and deciding not to drive. A domestic row or a confrontation at work inevitably causes tension, so the occasional state of mind when one is unable to concentrate totally on the considerable responsibility of driving a car safely must be recognised. It is inexcusable to succumb to the temptation of letting off steam by driving aggressively or too quickly. In the same way, speed limits must be observed no matter how late you may be for an appointment.

Be aware

No-one is likely to drive when they are ill, but even minor complaints can seriously affect ability behind the wheel. A cold can slow your reactions, dull judgement and make a person bad-tempered. Even a bad night's sleep might impair concentration. When you feel under the weather, only you can decide if you are fit enough to drive; if you decide that you are, drive with extra care.

Many drugs can impair your reactions, make you feel sleepy or affect your physical faculties in other ways, perhaps without your being fully aware of it. Doctors should warn patients about the side effects of any drugs they prescribe; if your doctor does not, you should ask. Driving under the influence of drugs can be as dangerous as driving with alcohol in your system: both are out of the question for all drivers.

Summary

- Take pride in being a *courteous and tolerant* driver at all times.
- Remember that the techniques of advanced driving can make your motoring *more enjoyable*.
- Always be aware of circumstances which affect your *state of mind*, and therefore your concentration or patience: sleepiness, illness, or stress after an argument can all impair your ability to drive safely.

5

STEERING

The importance of adopting the correct driving position was outlined in Chapter 3. To recap, you should sit neither hunched over the steering wheel nor too far from it. You should be comfortable, but not too relaxed. You should hold the wheel with your hands at the 'ten-to-two' or 'quarter-to-three' position, and your arms should be bent to an angle of between 90 and 120 degrees. With your hands correctly positioned, you are best placed to make a sudden yet accurate and controlled movement of the steering, should a violent change of direction be demanded. It is impossible for a driver with both hands close together gripping the '12 o'clock' part of the wheel, or one fondling the wheel with one hand at '6 o'clock', to cope properly with an emergency manoeuvre.

Feeding the wheel

Steering movements should be made by feeding the wheel through your hands. This is how the technique works. When turning right, for example, pull the rim down a few inches with the right hand and let it slide through the fingers of the left. As your right hand reaches the bottom of the natural arc, keep up the turning movement by bringing your left hand, now gripping the rim, upwards. At the same time move your right hand up ready to repeat the operation. If you are not used to steering this way you may find that your movements feel somewhat unco-ordinated, but it takes only a little practice to develop the technique into a neat, controlled movement which applies steering lock progressively while allowing you to retain a firm grip on the wheel at all times. They may not realise it, but a surprising number of people manage to let go of the wheel completely for long moments during normal driving.

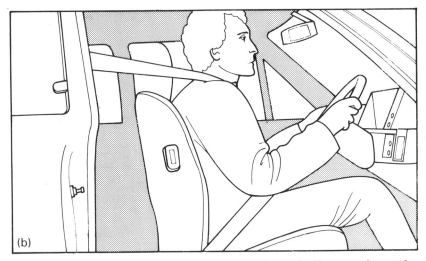

Your position at the wheel. The top picture shows the 'boy racer' straight arm technique – fine for the narrow confines of a racing car cockpit, but totally unsuitable for a road car. The picture below illustrates one of the most common bad driving positions: sitting too close to the wheel. This often reflects a lack of confidence and may be a pointer to short-sightedness. The correct position is shown in the above right picture. The arms and legs are comfortably positioned, with the hands falling naturally at the 'ten-to-two' or 'quarter-to-three' position.

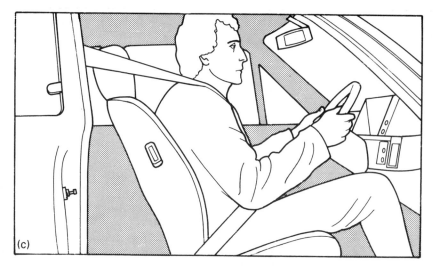

(c)

As you come out of a turn, straighten up by reversing the method. Do not allow either hand to stray beyond the '12 o'clock' position, because this greatly reduces the degree of fine control you have over the steering. Even when you have applied considerable lock through a tight turn, your hands should still remain opposite each other, ready to apply corrective lock if you skid or extra lock should it be needed.

As you come out of a bend it can be tempting to allow the steering's self-centring action to pull the wheel back to the straight-ahead position by letting the rim slip through your fingers. Advanced drivers do not do this because it has a serious disadvantage when sudden steering movement is necessary. Valuable fractions of a second are wasted regaining a grip on the wheel and then working out just where the front wheels are pointing in relation to the steering. Only during low-speed manoeuvring, perhaps when turning round in a car park, can this method be regarded as acceptable. Although it is never strictly necessary, it is acceptable when parking or reversing to take one hand past '12 o'clock' on the rim.

At all other times the 'crossed hands' style at the wheel should be avoided because it prevents you from being in perfect control of the steering. Racing drivers can be seen crossing their hands (at least in the days when the driver was visible in his car), but for them speed is of the essence, danger is a secondary consideration and there is room to make mistakes. None of these aspects apply on public roads.

Steering accurately

Many motorists do not take the trouble to judge accurately the width of their cars, showing that they imagine the vehicle to be three feet wider than it really is by giving an excessively wide berth to any obstacle. Acquiring a precise idea of your car's width and length enables you to negotiate a path through congested traffic more easily, or to squeeze into a tight parking spot which once would have looked too small. You can learn to steer accurately and judge the dimensions of your car by practising with markers in an empty car park on a Sunday morning. Once this art is perfected, do not exploit it unwisely by passing parked cars or overtaking with only inches to spare, or taking left-hand bends within a hair's breadth of the kerb.

Gentle but firm touch

As well as positioning the hands correctly, you should also grip the wheel in the right way. Timid or inexperienced drivers often grip the wheel so tightly that the whites of their knuckles show. Apart from being tiring, an excessively strong grip also tends to make steering movements coarser, which can cause the car to drift from side to side when cruising at 70mph on a motorway. With properly adjusted steering any car should run straight, but to do so it responds best to a light, but firm, hold. Most cars are influenced by strong cross-winds or by the buffeting which occurs when passing a large coach or truck on the motorway, and in these circumstances a gentle touch is best for applying tiny steering corrections. Steering a car is like horse riding: keep a firm but gentle hold on the reins. If perspiration makes a plastic steering wheel rim slippery, use a lace-on leather cover, or driving gloves thin enough to permit sensitive touch.

Never wear thick gloves when driving in winter before the heater has had a chance to warm the car through. They are clumsy, can affect your grip and tend to

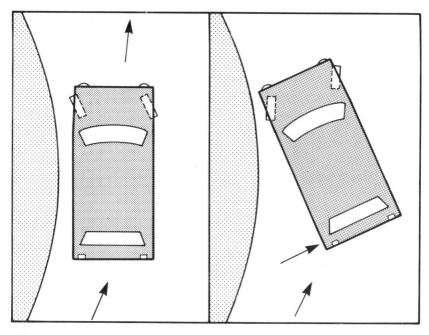

The position of a car's front wheels in an understeer situation (left) and an oversteer situation (right).

make your steering movements coarse, which in wet or icy conditions can lead to a skid. Since you are not such an alert driver when you are shivering, it is best to let the car warm up for five or ten minutes before setting out on a winter journey.

Sensitivity in steering is of crucial importance, especially if your car has power-assisted steering. Most systems are far more sophisticated than they used to be, some cars now having a degree of assistance which varies according to speed, but the driver may still be denied some of the all-important steering 'feel'. Messages through the steering about how the front wheels are reacting to the road surface give the experienced driver a great deal of useful information. Power-assisted steering, which seems to mask this feedback from the front wheels, must be treated with respect because it is all too easy for a sudden steering movement on a wet road to cause the front wheels to break grip and start a front-wheel skid. Artificial lightness should not be taken to mean that your car's road-holding is any better.

Basic handling

We cannot leave the subject of steering without discussing the much-quoted – and often misunderstood – terms of 'oversteer' and 'understeer'. These refer to the basic handling characteristics of a car, not to any action taken by the driver. Most cars, particularly those with front-wheel drive, tend to need more steering lock than might be expected to hold course through a bend, especially at higher speeds: this is understeer. Other cars, particularly rear-engined and many rear-wheel drive models, can need less steering lock than would be expected, requiring the driver to ease off the steering slightly to keep the car on course: this is oversteer. The 'under' and 'over' refer to how the car responds to being deflected from the straight and narrow by the steering.

Summary

- Always steer by *feeding the wheel* through your hands, so that you have at least one hand gripping the rim at all times; crossing the hands is not the best way to control the steering.
- Learn to steer *accurately* with a clear idea of your car's width; avoid *coarse movements* which in poor conditions may cause the front wheels to skid.
- Hold the wheel with a *gentle but firm touch*, for maximum sensitivity.

6

BRAKING

Proper use of the brakes is an integral part of advanced driving and involves rather more than simply pressing the pedal when you want to slow down or stop. Before looking at the subtleties of braking technique in detail, it is first necessary to deal with the brakes themselves.

Types of brakes

Most cars in regular use have disc brakes at the front and drum brakes at the rear; more expensive cars with higher performance have disc brakes on all four wheels. Although many people believe that disc brakes offer better stopping power, they are not intrinsically more powerful than the old-fashioned drum type. It is their resistance to fade which makes the disc brake superior; this explains why they are almost universally fitted at the front, since weight transfer when braking means that the front wheels provide as much as 70 per cent of the stopping effort.

A brake of any type heats up when it is used, and if used frequently and heavily it will heat up to the point where braking power diminishes – 'fades' – or even disappears altogether. It is possible to drive for a lifetime without ever experiencing fade but it can arise when you most need the brakes, such as through a series of hairpin bends on the descent from a mountain pass. You can detect brake fade from the extra pressure which begins to be needed on the pedal to achieve the same stopping power; in these circumstances it is best to stop to allow the brakes to cool down, for all braking response can be lost if the overheated surfaces are punished any further. Drum brakes fade more readily than discs because they disperse heat less efficiently.

Either type of brake, disc or drum, is capable of locking a wheel if you hit the pedal hard enough, even on a

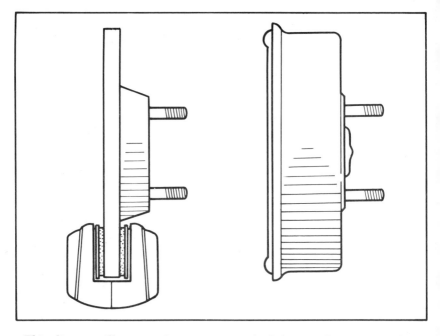

This diagram illustrates how more air (shaded area) flows over a disc brake (left) than over a drum brake. It is the cooling effect of this air which makes discs less prone to 'brake fade'.

dry road. The grip of the tyres, not the brakes themselves, determines how effectively a car stops in an emergency. A set of four modern tyres, each with a contact area the size of a man's shoe sole, does a remarkable job in keeping a car weighing a ton or two on the road.

Even the best tyres can be pushed beyond their limit. They will begin to lose their grip, lock up and start skidding if the brake pedal is pushed too hard, particularly on a wet road. A car with locked wheels cannot stop at anywhere near the best possible rate, and may even feel as if it is gaining speed. Since the most powerful braking occurs just before the wheels lock up, it is worth developing a feel for this moment in your own car, although the public road is not the place to practise. A skid pan or disused airfield are suitable places, but in the absence of these your local road safety officer may have a suggestion. Practise emergency stops at progressively higher speeds, as this experience will be invaluable should a real emergency occur.

Cadence braking

Advanced drivers should be familiar with the dabbing technique – 'cadence' braking – which keeps the wheels rolling for optimum braking in an emergency stop. This is how it works. When the driver feels one or more wheels begin to lock, he momentarily releases the pressure on the brake pedal to allow the locked wheels to rotate again, then re-applies pressure for maximum stopping power. The process may need to be repeated several times before the car comes to rest. With practice, this on-off technique can be refined to the point where you can keep the wheels almost continuously gripping at that threshold of lock-up where the car stops most efficiently. An advanced driver should never demand so much of his brakes in normal use that cadence braking is necessary, but in an emergency on a slippery surface its use could avoid an accident.

An increasing number of new cars, including some relatively ordinary models, are fitted with an Automatic Braking System (ABS), otherwise known as anti-lock brakes. In effect, these do the cadence braking for you, although more quickly and efficiently than any driver could manage. Sensors and pressure-limiting valves, controlled by computer, do the work of the human brain and foot, their operation being felt as a series of pulses through the brake pedal. This technical advance is a valuable safety aid, although no driver of a car with ABS should ever be lulled into a false sense of security, or abuse the system by relying on it to make quicker progress when conditions are poor. An advanced driver ought to be able to drive for years without ever using his car's ABS.

The real experts in the techique of cadence braking are rally drivers who time their hard pushes on the brake pedal to coincide with the spring frequency of the front suspension, thereby taking advantage of the 'nose-dive' characteristic inherent in most cars. Braking imposes extra load on the front of the car, pushing it down on its springs and increasing the weight on the front tyres. With the front tyres doing most of the work under braking, their grip is usefully improved. When the brake is released the front of the car lifts momentarily and then bounces down as the springs compress again. At this moment the pedal is pushed hard again, the front tyres grip better because of the increased load and the wheels are less likely to lock. With practice, really skilled drivers can time their pedal movements to coincide perfectly with the car's nose-dive action. This technique is highly specialised, suitable only after considerable private practice, and appropriate on the road only in dire emergency.

The essential thing is to remember that the brakes stop the wheels, but that the tyres stop the car. You should always know you car's braking capabilities and learn to recognise its limits of adhesion on all kinds of road surface.

Braking distance

Just as important is an understanding of the distance needed to stop a car from any speed. As the frequency of nose-to-tail accidents on busy motorways shows, many motorists seem to have little idea of how much room is needed to stop a car, even in good conditions. The old rule of thumb for stopping distance, 'one car's length for every 10mph', in fact represents only thinking distance, which is only part of the picture. A mere 90 feet at 60mph, which this misconception suggests, would be adequate if the car in front also slows down at a normal rate, but just occasionally it stops a good deal quicker if it hits a vehicle ahead. In emergencies you need at least twice as much space between you to pull up.

The distance required to stop increases in indirect proportion to speed: double your speed from 30mph to 60mph and you will need *four* times the braking distance. The advanced motorist will learn to judge safe braking distances automatically, but there is a useful formula to remember if in doubt: square the speed and divide by 20 to get the distance in feet. For 60mph, therefore, $60 \times 60 = 3600 \div 20 = 180$ feet – in other words, exactly double what the old rule suggests. And this formula is appropriate to a good car on a dry road surface. Braking distance increases dramatically in the wet, or even after a light shower on the

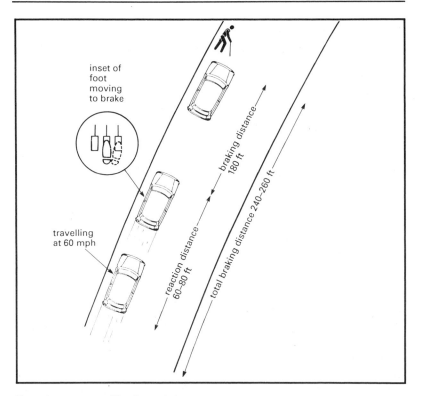

inset of
foot
moving
to brake

travelling
at 60 mph

reaction distance
60–80 ft

braking distance
180 ft

total braking distance 240–260 ft

Reaction time and braking distance. To ensure a safe braking distance, a useful formula to remember is: square the speed and divide by 20 to get the distance in feet. At 60mph, therefore, 60 × 60 = 3600 ÷ 20 = 180 feet. To this must be added an allowance for reaction time, which, at this speed, would mean an additional 60–80 feet. The total braking distance for a car travelling at 60mph is, therefore, 240–260 feet.

slippery film of oil, dust and rubber which coats roads in summer. As for snow and ice, the figures rise so alarmingly that someone idiotic enough to be travelling at 60mph could take a third of a mile to stop.

To these calculations must be added the thinking distance. Even people with the sharpest reactions need time for their first sight of a hazard ahead to produce an order from the brain to the foot, which must then move from the accelerator pedal to the brake and start applying pressure. Someone who can do all this in half a second has superb reactions, yet in this time a car travelling at 30mph moves 22 feet, and one travelling at 60mph moves 44 feet. For most drivers, with slower reactions, thinking distance at 60mph is nearer 60–80 feet. This is a significant figure to be added to actual braking distance.

Avoiding fierce braking

The importance of travelling at a safe distance behind the vehicle in front must always be stressed, but for advanced drivers this becomes second nature. As a result, anyone who has acquired the skills of advanced motoring will seldom find it necessary to brake fiercely. Unnecessarily heavy braking is uncomfortable for passengers, wears out brake pads and tyres more quickly and can alarm other drivers.

Good braking procedure is simple: you should apply the brakes smoothly and progressively for about two-thirds to three-quarters of the distance in which you wish to stop, easing up on the pressure for the last third to a quarter. Gentler braking for the last section leaves a margin if you have miscalculated or need to stop sooner than you expect, perhaps if the man ahead pulls up short of the Stop line.

A driver who keeps his brakes on quite hard until the car stops makes life uncomfortable for his passengers, even though he may not notice the jolt to standstill himself. Advanced drivers come to a stop smoothly and gently by slackening the pressure on the brake pedal for the last 10mph or so, and then for the last few feet easing back still further so that the car rolls to a halt under the lightest touch of the pedal. Any good chauffeur knows that practice can make the moment of stopping imperceptible. You can discover whether you have achieved such a fine touch with the brakes by glancing out of the corner of your eye to see whether your passenger's head nods forward when the car stops.

Brake in a straight line

Braking through a corner is a cardinal sin which most drivers do much of the time. Only the excellent handling qualities of modern cars allow drivers to get away with this continually without incident. Except when moving slowly, braking should always be carried out with the car travelling in a straight line. Sometimes braking in a bend may seem unavoidable, but more often than not you are guilty of poor anticipation if you need to do it.

It is easy to cause a skid by braking on a bend when driving at all quickly, particularly in the wet. This occurs because centrifugal force makes the body roll towards the outside of a corner, imposing more load on the outer tyres and removing weight from the inner tyres, which thereby become more prone to locking up and precipitating a skid. In extreme circumstances, braking on a corner can exceed the limit of a tyre's adhesion. If 80 per cent of a tyre's adhesive ability is being used to maintain course round a corner and the driver suddenly asks for another 40 per cent by braking suddenly, the tyre will be unable to cope. The result will be a skid. There used to be a time when drivers were all too aware of the limitations of a car's handling, but modern suspension and tyre design enable cars to travel round corners very much more quickly. When sudden braking finds today's higher road-holding limits, the result can be frightening, or worse still can end in a crash.

Brake failure

The almost universal adoption of dual-circuit braking systems by car manufacturers means that complete brake failure is very rare nowadays, but it can still occur. If the cause is a slow leak of hydraulic fluid you may have some warning from the pedal, which will travel further and may feel spongy. Pumping hard on the pedal to bring more fluid from the reservoir into the system can produce a temporary improvement, but the cause must be rectified before you lose the brakes altogether.

The most alarming kind of brake failure is when there is no warning, just the awful realisation that the pedal produces no response. You must do what you can with the hand-brake (which has a separate mechanical, not hydraulic, linkage) and use the engine to help slow down the car by dropping through the gears as quickly as possible without revving up between each down-change. With luck and skill, you may be able to steer out of trouble. Few drivers ever experience this frightening occurrence, but should it happen and you keep your wits about you the hand-brake and gears might get you out of trouble.

Although disc brakes have reduced the fade problem, their performance can suffer because they are exposed to the elements. If water builds up between disc and pad on a long motorway drive through a rainstorm, there can be a momentary lack of response when eventually you apply the brakes. It is wise to dab the brakes occasionally to keep them clean if you drive many miles in torrential rain without using them, but only when no cars are behind.

A few drivers with automatic transmission in their cars sometimes use the left foot to operate brakes, but this really is not sensible. Your early training as a driver makes right-foot braking an almost instinctive action, and in an emergency you could find your feet confused. You may lock up the brakes with both feet on the pedal, or even press on the accelerator with the right foot at the same time as using your left foot on the brake.

Racing drivers use the 'heel and toe' technique – pivoting the right foot so that the heel presses the throttle at the same time as the ball of the foot operates the brake – to achieve clean and swift changes down through the gears as they approach a corner on the track. Some drivers put this into practice on the road, but there is little point. The fractions of a second saved on the track mean nothing on the public highway, and it is always possible that you may not brake properly while trying to use two pedals with one foot. It may seem clever to 'heel and toe', but it has little relevance in everyday driving. In any case, the pedals in most cars are not ideally arranged for this technique.

Other drivers

Finally, before we leave the subject of braking, keep an eye on the other drivers around you. Be prepared for the driver in front to pull up sharply without any obvious reason by allowing even more braking distance in case he miscalculates. Look out, too, for the crumpled old banger looming up in your interior mirror, and allow for the fact that his brakes might not be as good as yours. And try to give extra warning to a driver who 'rides' your back bumper by braking earlier than usual, starting with a light touch on the brake pedal to bring on your brake lights. Leave yourself more braking distance than usual so that your own gentle braking can be used to give the thoughtless driver behind more stopping distance.

Summary

- Familiarise yourself with your car's braking ability, and practise *cadence braking* to avoid locking the wheels in an emergency.
- Always be aware of the *braking distance* you need at any speed, and allow for *thinking distance* too in the gap you leave for the vehicle in front.
- Avoid fierce braking. Brake *smoothly and progressively* over the first two-thirds or so of your braking period, then release the pressure gradually so that you come to a stop gently.
- Except at low speed, try to brake in a *straight line*, since sudden braking on a corner can cause a skid.
- Allow for *other drivers* around you in your use of the brakes.

7

ACCELERATION AND ECONOMY

There is a great deal more to using a car's power than meets the eye. A car should not be driven hard or its performance abused, but power used wisely, in the right place at the right time, can be the safest course of action. When confronted with a hazard, it can be preferable to accelerate away rather than brake or steer your way out of trouble. Considering the efforts of car manufacturers to improve performance, and the importance which many car buyers attach to it, it is surprising how rarely this response is used by drivers. Moments do arise, such as during overtaking, when a car should be driven to the full extent of its potential, as more force with the right foot could keep a driver out of trouble rather than getting him into it.

Acceleration and overtaking

Unless you are travelling on a motorway or a dual carriageway, you have to move to the 'wrong' side of the road when you wish to overtake. This is an extremely dangerous place to be, and the longer you are there the longer you are exposed to the possibility of meeting oncoming traffic. It is absolutely essential to know exactly your car's acceleration potential, because you can find yourself in serious trouble if you expect more than it can give.

If you feel that you need to explore the capabilities of your car, find a deserted stretch of road with no low speed limits and put your car through its paces. If the car's instruments include a rev counter, use this to discover the maximum speeds possible in the lower gears; if there is no rev counter, the manufacturer's handbook will tell you the maximum speeds possible in each gear. Try a couple of runs to find out what the car can take so that you know how the engine sounds when it is close to its limit. You will probably be surprised just how much acceleration is available, even from a modest car, and it will give you a clear idea of what power to expect when you really need it.

You will normally not need to push the car to its maximum when you overtake, but you should still get by as quickly as seems safe and reasonable, from both your own point of view and that of the overtaken driver. Always select the right gear before starting to overtake. With a five-speed gearbox this is usually fourth or third, but second may be better if the vehicle ahead of you is travelling quite slowly (many cars can exceed 60mph in this gear). With a four-speed gearbox, third is the usual overtaking gear but many situations will demand second.

As you start the manoeuvre, apply the power smoothly; opening the throttle sharply is clumsy, and on a slippery road could cause the wheels to break traction (creating the wheelspin that can lead to a skid). It ought to be possible to complete the passing manoeuvre without changing up a gear until you have returned safely to the left-hand side of the road. If you do have to change up while you are overtaking, do so swiftly but smoothly, since releasing the clutch savagely can have the same effect as depressing the accelerator too suddenly.

Acceleration sense and economy

Acceleration sense must be acquired by every driver. This is the ability to judge, almost as second nature, whether you can safely carry out a manoeuvre and, having decided that you can, to make full use of your car's power while still driving safely. Acceleration sense comes only from experience and familiarity with the car you drive. Sensitivity in controlling the throttle is required to produce good acceleration sense, and for this reason you should always wear sensible shoes when driving. Many advanced drivers adopt the excellent habit of keeping a pair of thin-soled shoes in the car especially for driving so that they can exercise a delicate touch on the accelerator.

The way you drive has a dramatic effect on fuel economy, which is important to most of us. Without reducing journey times, an average motorist covering 12,000 miles annually could save as much as £100 a year on fuel by showing more sensitivity in his use of brake and accelerator pedals. Ramming the accelerator to the floor, revving too high and driving impatiently all use up fuel more quickly. Some drivers could also make a significant saving by abandoning the pointless habit of revving up the engine with the gearbox in neutral.

If road conditions are bad enough, harsh use of the accelerator can cause an accident. Most cars have sufficient power to spin the wheels if the road is wet enough. Even when moving off at traffic lights or from junctions, the combination of releasing the clutch too suddenly and applying too much pressure on the throttle can set the wheels spinning. The reaction of a front-wheel drive car will be a shudder, the noise of the engine racing and possibly some unnerving side-to-side tugging through the steering. A rear-wheel drive car can react more unpredictably, for wheelspin at the back can cause the car's tail end to start sliding round in a slow-motion skid which must be corrected with opposite lock steering. In all cars, whether the power goes through the front or rear wheels, your action should be to take your foot off the throttle and then re-apply power more gently.

Warming the engine

Before we leave the subject of acceleration, it should be mentioned that your car may respond less willingly before its engine has warmed up. Sudden opening of the throttle too soon after a cold start in the morning may cause the engine to falter, as if it is gasping for breath, or in an extreme case may even result in a stall. Having a manual choke on the wrong setting will make the engine even more sluggish. It is even more important than normal, therefore, to operate the accelerator progressively, and avoid demanding more from the engine than it is capable of giving. Be especially vigilant when pulling away from junctions and at roundabouts, especially if traffic is heavy. No car likes to be revved hard before its oil has had a chance to warm up, so let it reach running temperature in its own time.

Summary

- Become familiar with your car's *acceleration* ability, but use all the power available only when absolutely necessary. Develop your *acceleration sense* so you know instinctively when a manoeuvre, such as overtaking, can be carried out safely.
- Use as much power (in the most suitable gear) as seems safe and reasonable when *overtaking*.
- Treat the *accelerator pedal* sensitively; smooth and progressive acceleration is safer than sudden movement on the throttle, and you use less fuel too.

OBSERVATION

To be an advanced driver you need to become a skilled observer. Good powers of observation, which demand practice and thought, can keep you out of trouble in 90 per cent of all potentially dangerous incidents. You need to absorb all the information you see around and ahead of you when you drive, and select what is useful. All drivers do this to a certain extent, but the real value of skilled observation does not come until it has been developed into an art. Just as a ship's master reads his chart in difficult waters, you must read the road ahead so that you can anticipate potential dangers.

Your eyesight

Making sure that your vision is satisfactory is the first step you must take. Not only do an alarming number of drivers have eyesight shortcomings, but many of them are also totally unaware that anything is wrong. Eyesight usually deteriorates so gradually that a person who 20 years ago read a number-plate without difficulty when passing his test may now be suffering from a potentially dangerous defect in his vision, and possibly compensating for it subconsciously. Many people who try to avoid driving at night, because they are not happy about their vision in the darkness, ought to acknowledge that their daylight vision might also be less than perfect.

Reading a number-plate for the requirements of the Government test is not demanding enough. The standard is to be able to read a number-plate with the old 3½in letters at a distance of 75 feet (22.86 metres), or a plate with the newer 3⅛in letters at a distance of 67 feet (20.42 metres). It is possible to pass this requirement with little or no sharp sight in one eye, yet such a serious defect prevents good judgement of distance. Tunnel vision, the tendency to concentrate only on the view directly ahead and remain oblivious to anything more than a few degrees to the side, also does not stop you reading a number-plate at 25 yards, yet it seriously restricts the powers of observation which every driver must have.

Good peripheral sight is essential in order to see what is happening at each side of the car. Long sight and short sight are extremely common (and proportionately worse at night), but too many drivers remain unaware of it until eventually they are forced to have an eye-test. Colour blindness also causes serious problems, particularly if it takes the form of an inability to distinguish red; as well as brake lights and traffic lights, red is used for all danger signs on the road. If you have not been to an optician for two years, it would be wise to go for a proper check whether or not you already wear spectacles. There will probably be nothing wrong; but if there is, it is better to find out now rather than after a possible serious accident caused by your defective sight.

If you need glasses for driving, wear them always. It is a good idea, too, to keep a pair of dark glasses in the car all the year round, for the glare from the setting sun in winter can be just as hard on the eyes as the brightness of a sunny day in summer. Economy is pointless, as it is with anything to do with road safety. Polarised glasses are the best, but try them in your car first to make sure that they do not excessively emphasise the stress patterns which can be seen in car windscreens when this type of glass is used. If you normally wear spectacles, the ideal is a second pair with tinted glass lenses. Sunglasses with cheap plastic lenses can scratch easily and make parts of your vision 'foggy', and they tend to impair your perception in shade.

Sunglasses are useful in reducing eyestrain, but never be tempted to wear them at night if you are bothered by dazzle. Glare from oncoming headlights is reduced, but so is your perception of everything else which is marginally lit. Failing to see a pedestrian, an unlit cyclist or even just the kerb could have fatal results. If your eyesight is good and oncoming headlights do dazzle you, you are probably making the elementary mistake of looking right at them. With a little willpower, you can train yourself to look away from the headlights and towards the nearside of the road

The importance of good eyesight. The top, left *picture shows the view from behind the wheel of a person with average eyesight. Everything is clear, and peripheral vision is adequate. The* centre, left *picture shows the effect of long-sightedness, with the foreground blurred and the distant objects in focus. Short-sightedness is even worse, as is illustrated by the* bottom, left *picture. Everything ahead of you is dangerously blurred. Tunnel vision (top) is a less common defect, but potentially disastrous. The view straight ahead is fine, but peripheral vision is badly affected. The hazards of such a defect need no elaboration. Finally, some people suffer from double vision, which can greatly affect your judgement on the road. If you suffer from these or other defects, it is in your own interest, as well as that of all other road users, to do something about it.*

instead. This ability comes naturally with plenty of night driving experience, and in time you will appreciate the headlights of passing traffic for that little bit of extra light they throw into your path. The inevitable reaction to headlights coming towards you is to concentrate your attention on the part of the road directly in front of your car illuminated by your own headlights. At all other times, however, you must look further ahead, day or night.

Where to look

Many inexperienced drivers spend most of their time behind the wheel looking at the part of the road immediately in front of them, thereby failing to notice sufficiently early the approach of junctions, roundabouts, parked cars and any other potential hazards. You should concentrate your gaze on a point some way ahead, while at the same time taking in events even further in the distance, closer to you and on either side.

This selective vision requires concentration and has to be developed with practice, so it is a good idea to train yourself to cast your eye over as wide a field of vision as possible. An advanced driver with excellent peripheral vision can often point out objects at the side of the road (such as a dog on the verge) that even his passengers have missed, while at the same time keeping the centre of his gaze focused on the road ahead. This centre of focus must be adjusted constantly according to speed and how far ahead the road is visible.

You must also be observant about what is going on behind you. The interior mirror must be used frequently, and always before you change course or speed, but you should not rely on this alone. Properly adjusted door or wing mirrors give you a broader field of vision behind, although there will always be some blind spots, notably just above your right shoulder and perhaps at the three-quarter rear position one each side (especially on a car with large metal panels at these points). If your car is inadequately equipped, advice about choosing mirrors to minimise these blind spots is contained in Chapter 3.

You must always allow for blind spots when checking the view in your mirrors. The advanced driver uses his mirrors so often that he should always be aware of the vehicles behind him, and should know when one is momentarily in a blind spot. Even so, the only way to ensure that you are never caught out by a car or motorcycle hidden in a blind spot and about to overtake is to cast a quick – and we really mean quick – glance over your right shoulder if all looks safe ahead. This is especially good practice when changing lanes on a motorway or dual carriageway, joining traffic flow from a slip road or changing lanes in a one-way system, as well as when pulling away from the side of the road. You need to be particularly vigilant about what might be lurking in a blind spot when you are travelling on a busy motorway; if a lane of traffic to your right is flowing only slightly faster than your lane, a car can be concealed in a blind spot for some time. Motorway accidents are often caused by a driver changing lanes without properly checking in his mirrors and over his shoulder whether it is safe to do so, and then moving broadside into another car.

You must be absolutely certain that no vehicles, people or animals are behind you when you need to reverse. If your car gives poor vision to the rear, get out first and walk around to have a look. To reverse blindly, hoping that nothing or no-one – a playing child, for example – is in the way, is unforgivable.

Selective observation

Being observant is essential to advanced driving, but the refinement of this skill comes in learning to be selective in your observation. When driving in a busy city centre, for example, you need to be able to distinguish what should be acted upon and what can be ignored. These are some pointers to give you an idea of the range of visual information which helps you to become a safer driver:

- Changing road surface: a sudden switch from a dull surface to a shiny one, or from a coarse surface to a smooth one, could mean that tyre grip will be reduced and stopping distance lengthened.
- Mud or gravel at farm or building site entrances can make the road more slippery.

- Telegraph poles changing course can indicate a bend in the road, but remember that occasionally the wires can track straight on while the road bends.
- Unexpected movements by parked vehicles must always be allowed for if you see a driver inside. The vehicle can suddenly move out into your path if the driver sets off without thinking, or the driver or a passenger might open a door and step out into your path.
- Cross-winds can blow through gaps between buildings or trees and buffet your car off its course if you are caught unawares.
- Give tradesmen's stationary vans a wide berth, especially on quiet roads, in case the driver gets out unexpectedly.
- Any parked vehicle can hide a pedestrian about to step out into the road, so it's a good idea to look for tell-tale feet visible underneath it; school buses and ice cream vans should be treated with particular care.
- Any pedestrian needs to be observed carefully. A child can dash into the road without looking and an old person, perhaps with failing eyesight or hearing, might not see you coming; a dog off a lead could do anything. Be especially careful in wet weather: a pedestrian is not always so careful when he is hurrying for shelter, or if his vision is restricted because he is keeping his head down against the rain.
- Always give a cyclist plenty of room. Riding a bicycle carefully is difficult in wind or rain, and not all cyclists are skilled on their machines. Always assume that a cyclist might wobble or steer round a drain or pothole just as you pass.
- You can glean plenty of information by observing other vehicles. A parked car with its reversing lights on is clearly about to move backwards. A puff from the exhaust of a parked car means that its driver has just started the engine and may pull out into your path. A puff from the exhaust of a lorry climbing a hill tells you that its driver has changed down and will be travelling even more slowly; if you are coming down a hill and see a slow-moving lorry climbing towards you, it could conceal a car whose driver is about to attempt

a rash overtaking manoeuvre. A decrepit car or van might have poor brakes. Give more room to the aggressive or sloppy driver; drop further back from a driver ahead trying to overtake when there is no opportunity, or a driver who is paying more attention to finding a particular address in town than he is to the road. If you are behind a bus, a passenger putting his hand up to the bell will give you advance warning that the bus is about to stop.

Anyone who has passed the Government driving test should have all road signs committed to memory, but it is still worth referring to the *Highway Code* periodically to check that you know all the warning signs (triangular), advisory ones (rectangular) and mandatory ones (circular). British roads are quite well provided with signs, all of which are erected by local authorities for a purpose; you should know at a glance what any sign is telling you.

No matter how experienced a driver you are, there is always room to improve your observation skills still further. Take pride in developing your own methods. At a familiar junction in town with a restricted view, for example, you might notice that reflections in a shop window act as mirrors and show you what otherwise invisible traffic is approaching. With this sort of keen observation, the advanced driver can always make his motoring that little bit safer.

Summary

- Observation depends upon *good eyesight*, so make sure that you have an eye-test frequently (at least every two years) even if you are confident that your vision has not deteriorated.
- *Concentrate your gaze* on a point some way ahead, while at the same time taking in events even further in the distance, closer to you and on either side.
- Develop the skills of *selective observation* so that you have an eye for any situation which might require action from you.
- Be particularly aware of *blind spots* when using your mirrors.

BENDS AND CORNERS

A driver never has anyone to blame but himself if he goes off the road on a bend. The results can be disastrous, especially if such foolhardy driving results in a collision with another vehicle. Yet drivers often do not regard themselves as being at fault – excuses may be given about adverse camber, the road being greasy or the curve tightening up unexpectedly. Any of these can be factors in an accident, but never the cause. The reason for going off the road always lies in bad driving in one form or another.

Cornering forces

It is worth analysing the forces which act on a car when it is steered round a corner. A car's momentum takes it in a straight line (just like a golf ball struck true and straight down the fairway) until the driver turns the steering wheel. The front wheels move to a position at an angle to the straight path they are following and the car starts to turn into the bend. At this point centrifugal force begins to act, trying to push the car outwards in the same way that a piece of string with a weight at the end tautens when you swing it round in the air. This force is felt inside the car as it pushes you sideways in your seat, away from the inside of the bend. A car with soft suspension also reacts by rolling down on its springs on the outer side.

The tyres have to work harder to resist centrifugal force as they are subjected to this curved path, and those on the driven wheels also have to deal with the business of transmitting power to the road. The faster a corner is taken, the harder the tyres have to work. It goes without saying that there comes a moment when a driver can ask too much of his tyres, causing them gradually to lose their grip; a skid will start and the car may run off the road.

The right course through a bend

Avoiding excessive speed through corners is quite obviously a prerequisite of safe driving, but it is important also to take bends as smoothly as possible. Smoothness allows a driver to corner at reasonable speed without putting too much stress on the tyres. One technique to make cornering that little bit smoother and safer is to 'straighten' a bend slightly, but without crossing the central line. Never cut across the inside of a bend because it could endanger or worry other road users. Just because you may have heard racing drivers talk about 'straightening' a bend does not mean that there is any virtue in dashing through corners; on a race circuit speed is the object, drivers can use the full width of the road and all the cars travel in the same direction. None of this applies on the public road. We are talking about a milder version of 'straightening' a bend, whereby it is permissible to make sensible use of the width of your side of the road to ease the curve and improve your view round it.

Let us take the example of a right-hand bend. To take the best line through, enter the bend well over to the left of the road, then gradually move a little towards the middle so that your offside wheels are close to the central white line as you pass the apex. By using this line, the widest possible arc, you gain the best and earliest view out of the bend and reduce the centrifugal force on the tyres. All of this should be done with such subtlety that it is really not obvious to other road users; this technique should never be exaggerated, and you should err towards a regular line when there is other traffic about. If someone is stupid enough to attempt to overtake you through a corner, keep well to the nearside and slow down to give him more margin if his error gets him into difficulties with oncoming traffic.

Cornering procedure in detail

The generalisations which can be made about procedure

through bends are limited, but on right-hand bends this should be your basic programme:

- As the bend approaches, check your mirror in case someone is coming up behind or even contemplating nipping by before – or, worse still, through – the corner.
- Judge the speed at which you should take the bend and carry out any braking necessary to slow down to that speed while the car is still moving in a straight line. Your speed should be such that you can always pull up within the distance you can see to be clear.
- While you are still travelling in a straight line, change down to a lower gear if it seems necessary so that acceleration is available as you leave the bend.
- Bear in mind the racing driver's adage, 'in slow, out fast', although do not place too much emphasis on the 'fast'.
- Start steering into the curve, taking care to make a smooth movement rather than a vicious tug at the wheel which will jerk the car into the bend.
- Press the accelerator slightly as the car responds to the steering. Any car will feel steadier under a little power rather than a trailing throttle, but this must be done very gently and smoothly.
- Look towards and past the apex to check that the exit is clear. Throughout the corner you should always be driving at a speed which allows you to brake to a standstill within the distance you can see.
- Push the throttle more firmly so that you can accelerate smoothly out of the bend as you pass the apex. This should be done well within the capabilities of your car, as too much power will overload the tyres and cause them to slide, especially if the road is wet. Remember that extra power may cause the car to run a little wide, so compensate as you steer through.

The reverse applies through a left-hand bend: make your approach towards the middle of the road while staying on the correct side of the central line, move over towards the nearside at the apex and then gradually ease back to your correct position, a few feet from the verge, at the end of the bend.

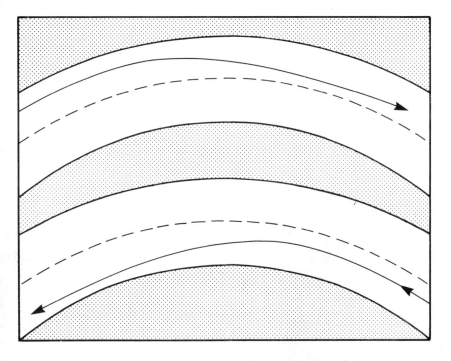

The optimum line for negotiating a right- or left-hand bend on a two-way road. 'Straightening' the curve in this way removes some of the danger from bends in roads, but should not be attempted if it involves changing lanes with other traffic nearby – and don't cross the central line unless you are quite certain that there is no car coming the other way.

Braking on a bend

You should always avoid braking on a bend, but there will be occasions when there is no option. A pedestrian may step out into your path or you may overestimate the safe speed. When it is necessary to brake, apply pressure as lightly as possible to the pedal to avoid asking too much from the tyres. If there is room, try to straighten the steering just before you brake, then turn again as you take your foot off the pedal.

You may be faced with a situation where heavy braking is necessary on a corner, although the advanced driver should seldom need to do so. He will have correctly judged the safe speed for the conditions, remembering that it is better to arrive at a corner too slowly than too quickly. He will have carefully assessed the road ahead as he approaches the corner and drives through it, making allowances for any pedestrains or vehicles likely to wander into his path. He will also have allowed for the bend tightening up or leading directly into another bend beyond his line of sight. All the possibilities will have dictated a conservative and safe speed into the corner, whether it is a completely open curve on a main road or a tight bend bordered by tall hedges on a country lane.

The unexpected can lie around any corner, and usually results from a driver being guilty of miscalculating the vehicle's speed so that there is difficulty in stopping when faced with a broken-down car, a tractor or a loose animal. The unexpected, however, could be another driver approaching on the wrong side of the road or, worse still, having an accident. It is better to try to steer away from such an alarming hazard rather than to brake on the corner. As well as increasing the chances of your own car skidding, braking can often leave you well placed to be struck by the other vehicle. Steering away from it provides a better chance of missing it altogether or perhaps receiving just a glancing blow. Never brake hard and steer at the same time.

If a car in front of you travelling in the same direction starts to slide, it is best to try to brake first to wipe off some speed (remembering the dangers involved in braking heavily while cornering), then prepare to steer to avoid the car. Keep an eye on its movement all the time: depending on the car's characteristics and the driver's action, it might plough off or spin towards the outside of the corner, or alternatively spin off towards the apex. With good judgement, you might be able to steer whichever side of the car offers the best path through if for any reason you cannot pull up first.

Summary

- Always *steer smoothly* through a corner, and slightly *straighten* a bend (without crossing the central white line) to improve your view and to reduce the stress on your car's tyres.

- Follow the correct *cornering procedure*: judge the safe speed for the corner, brake and change down to a lower gear if necessary while still moving in a straight line, and apply the power gently once you have entered the curve.
- Avoid *braking in a bend*; bear in mind the extra force on the tyres caused by braking while steering if a miscalculation or an emergency makes it necessary to brake on a corner.

10

JUNCTIONS

Extra risks face motorists wherever roads meet and diverge, whether at crossroads, T-junctions, roundabouts or forks, but by using the techniques of advanced driving and applying a systematic approach, junctions can be dealt with as safely as any other part of the road system. Accidents do not 'just happen' of their own accord – they are caused by bad driving. While you should always take extra care at junctions, you must recognise that they present an ideal opportunity for other road users to cause trouble. We have all seen other drivers adopt their own odd ways of approaching junctions and navigating their way through them. Be on your guard, therefore, for what a road safety expert might describe as 'an accident waiting to happen'.

Crossroads

The most opportunities for error, whether on your part or another road user's, occur at crossroads. When you are approaching on the minor route, or when neither route has precedence, plan ahead and be prepared to stop even though the signs may tell you only to give way. If your side of the road is wide enough for two lanes of traffic, ensure that you start moving into the correct one at an early stage after first checking your mirror and signalling accordingly. Stay in the left-hand lane if you intend to go straight across unless lane markings tell you to do otherwise, since keeping in the right-hand lane can dangerously mislead other motorists; besides, the right-hand lane at many crossroads is arranged so that travelling straight on inconveniences or even endangers other road users as you slot back into a single line of traffic. Even if there is insufficient room for doubling up the traffic lanes, it is still

The sign says 'Give Way' but, as is clear from this picture, it is often better, even necessary, to come to a halt. A surprisingly high number of accidents occur at points like this, whereas sensible driving would avoid trouble. Advanced motorists think about these situations in advance.

better to edge over to the side corresponding with the route you will follow as you leave the junction.

Straight ahead or turning left

When planning to go straight ahead or turning left, the procedure is relatively simple: wait until the road is clear to right and left, check that nothing is approaching from the opposite minor road and accelerate smartly away. Always watch, however, for one common cause of accidents. An oncoming vehicle signalling to turn left will lead you to expect it to turn off at the crossroads and not interfere with your intended path, but indicators can be left on by mistake. The driver may be planning to go straight ahead without realising that he is telling other road users otherwise. Never assume that a vehicle will turn until you actually see the driver begin moving into another road. If you pull out in front of him and cause a collision, the law would be unlikely to favour you.

Try to keep impatience under control when you are trying to turn left and traffic is heavy. A gap might look big enough for you to slip into if you accelerate hard enough and the driver behind slows down, but do not do it. Apart from being dangerous when the margins are slender, this sort of driving is discourteous. An accident could happen if the other driver is slow to react, if your engine falters or if you simply misjudge your move. This is a quite unnecessary risk just for the sake of shaving a few seconds off your journey time. Everyone knows the saying: it is better to be a few minutes late in this world than a few years early in the next.

Turning right

Right turns at crossroads can be more complicated, although they are governed by the same rules about not pushing in or taking indicator signals for granted. There can be confusion if opposing traffic is also turning right as drivers decide whether to pass offside-to-offside or vice versa. Half of the country's drivers seem to favour one way, the other half the other. However, there is only one safe rule, and that is to pass offside-to-offside; in other words, pass behind an opposing vehicle waiting to turn right. Do otherwise only when road markings or the junction layout dictate it. Some drivers seem to object to this procedure because it can limit the number of vehicles able to get through a right turn in one traffic light sequence, as well as requiring a gap to be left in an opposing line of vehicles waiting to turn right, but it is much safer. It means that each driver has a clearer view down the road ahead as he makes his turn. The nearside-to-nearside approach, where vehicles turn across the bows of the opposing line of traffic, forces each driver to nose out blindly across the traffic stream, greatly increasing the chances of an accident. It is hardly surprising that so many collisions happen when a driver is turning right.

The correct (below, right) and incorrect (above, right) procedure for turning right on a two-way road when faced with an oncoming car with the same intention, whenever possible. The lower diagram clearly illustrates how severely the 'nearside to nearside' method restricts your vision.

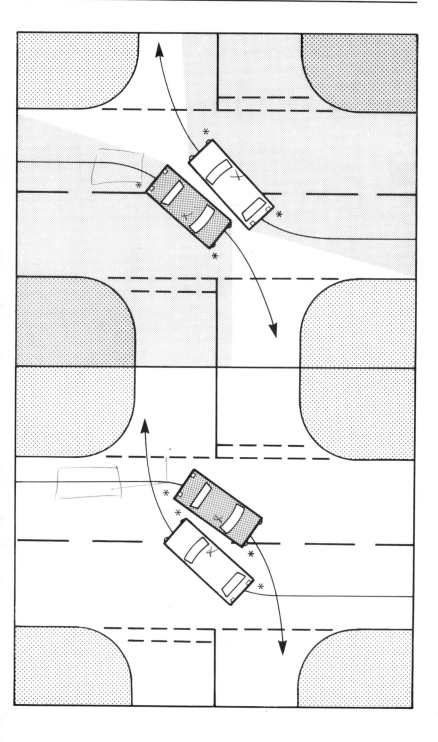

Courtesy at the crossroads

Using the more major of the two routes at a crossroads does not entitle you to drive as you like. Show courtesy and consideration to other road users, but not so excessively that you put politeness before practicality. By all means let someone out of a side turning if it is safe for you to do so, but it is dangerous and disruptive of traffic flow if you have to cause other drivers behind to brake. Misplaced courtesy can cause accidents if drivers around you are not expecting it. Let someone trying to pull out of a side road wait a little longer if you are in any doubt.

Traffic lights

Never take advantage of traffic light changes to try to nip through a junction and save yourself time. An alarming number of accidents in our towns and cities are caused by drivers trying rashly to save a few seconds, and the victims are often pedestrians. You should stop if you can reasonably do so when green changes to amber, and you must certainly never pass through the lights after amber has changed to red. Nor should you anticipate the change to green by moving away on red and amber; by all means keep an eye on the lights controlling the routes crossing your path so that you have advance warning of when your lights are to change, but do not use this to take liberties with the lights.

Since local authorities do not usually give much warning of filter lights ahead, sooner or later on an unfamiliar road you will probably find yourself sitting at a green left-turn filter when you want to go straight on. Even a brief pause will probably bring the sound of horns from behind. You could sit there waiting for the all-green phase, but it is far less selfish to make the turn and find an alternative way of getting back on to your route.

T-junctions

The rules outlined for procedure at crossroads apply equally to T-junctions: do not muscle your way into traffic flow on the assumption that other drivers will slow down for you, and always be aware that the vehicle with its indicator flashing may not make the turn out of your path which you expect it to.

Many T-junctions have a mini slip-road so that you can merge more easily with the traffic flowing on the main road. In fact they are often designed only to avoid a slow-speed 90-degree turn on to a busy main road, and generally do not offer sufficient width or length to allow you to reach the speed of the main traffic flow before you slot in. Treat these slip-roads with care: hold back if you have any doubts and wait for a suitable break in the traffic. All the same, do not be too timid at those slip-roads which are wide and long enough to work well. Use them as they are intended to be used, like a motorway slip-road. If you do come across an over-cautious driver who has stopped at the end of the slip-road waiting for a break in the traffic, accelerate smartly and move out into the main road early, provided that it is safe to do so, in order to be in the main stream before you pass the stationary vehicle.

Roundabouts

Hanging back at roundabouts can be just as unnecessary. You should strike the right balance between reserve and haste by making a decisive, safe entry into the traffic flow. Large roundabouts carry fast-moving traffic but often provide enough width for you to move into the nearside lane and build up your speed to match the flow of traffic around you. Small roundabouts have less acceleration space, but you need less room because traffic moves more slowly. Roundabouts are designed for maximum flow and easy entry at junctions where traffic is heavy, so do not queue unthinkingly at the approach roads. When traffic is light enough, it should be possible to enter a roundabout where visibility is good only with a reasonable reduction in speed and a change to a lower gear, all the time checking as you run up to the entry point that no vehicles are coming from the right. Where walls or hedges obscure visibility it may be necessary to slow down almost to a stop. Except where the priorities are marked differently, traffic on a roundabout has right of way.

Priority is sometimes given to a major route passing

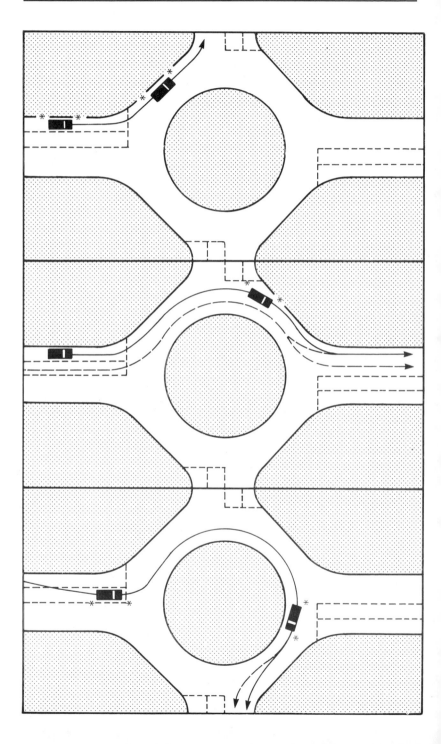

through a roundabout, so that drivers already on the roundabout have to give way when they meet this route. Changed priority is made to help speed traffic flow, but for a driver unfamiliar with the area the need to give way to traffic entering the roundabout can cause a moment's confusion. The advanced driver's observation skills should always alert him well ahead to an unusual circumstance such as this, but the risk can be reduced by keeping in your correct lane and remembering signalling procedures so that drivers around you are aware of your intentions.

Mini-roundabouts, especially those where there is a tight complex of two or three, can cause temporary confusion when you first meet unfamiliar ones, but the extra caution they require is sometimes regarded as their benefit. Since so many drivers are unsure of the procedure on them, traffic is slowed down to a safer speed. Except in the rare instances where road markings indicate differently, treat complexes of mini-roundabouts just like any other roundabout by giving way to vehicles coming from your right. Where a mini-roundabout is marked just by white lines on the road, never succumb to the temptation to cut across the island, even if there is no traffic about.

On all normal roundabouts you should keep to the established procedure outlined in the *Highway Code* unless lane markings tell you to do differently. If you plan to take the first exit, you should keep to the left and signal a left turn on your approach, keeping the indicator going until you leave the roundabout. If you plan to go more or less straight across, still keep to the left on your approach and through the roundabout, signalling a left turn after you have passed the exit before the one you intend to take. Your anticipation as an advanced driver should have given you plenty of time to move into the left lane on your

How to tackle a roundabout. Notice that if you intend to take the first exit (top, left) or the second (centre, left) then the inside lane is for you, because you will not then have to change lanes whilst going round. However, the outside lane (bottom, left) is the right one for you if you are to take the third exit. Always signal your intentions clearly, but not too soon, as you can easily confuse those behind you. However, with signalling, common sense must prevail.

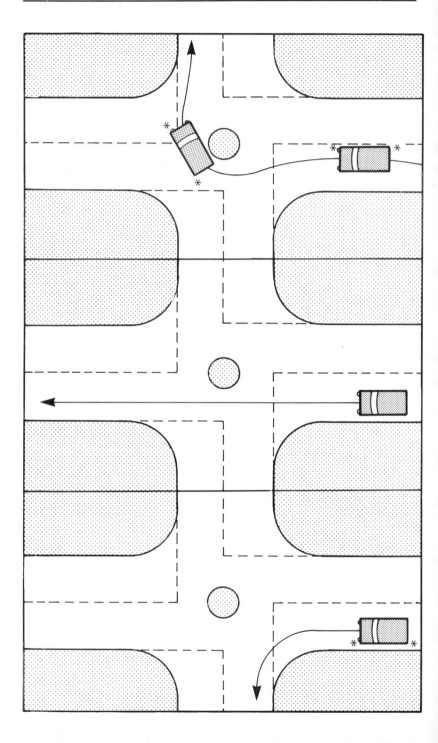

approach to the roundabout, but in very heavy traffic you might be obliged to stay over to the right; if this is the case, hold your course until you need to signal left and move over for your exit, taking care not to cut in front of any other vehicles. For exits more than 180 degrees round the roundabout, take the right-hand lane on your approach and signal a right turn before you enter the roundabout. Keep the indicator going until you pass the exit before the one you want, at which point starting signalling left and move over for your exit.

Summary

- Remember that all junctions create *extra danger*: always signal your intentions well in advance, take up the correct position on the road and move off only when you are certain it is safe to do so.
- When turning left or going straight across at a *crossroads*, do not endanger other road users by trying to shoulder into the flow of traffic, and never assume that a vehicle will follow the path suggested by its indicator signals.
- When *turning right* at a crossroads, pass oncoming vehicles also turning right offside-to-offside, unless road markings or junction layout dictate otherwise.
- Always use the correct lane and signalling procedure when approaching and negotiating *roundabouts*; your entry to a roundabout should be carefully judged, decisive and safe.

How to negotiate a mini-roundabout. The procedure for taking the first exit (top, left) is much the same as an ordinary left turn, though extra care must be taken to watch for traffic coming from the right. For the second exit (centre, left), no change of course should be necessary, though caution should again be exercised in regard to traffic from both right and left. The third exit is taken in exactly the same way as a full-size roundabout.

11

SIGNALS

When you are driving you use signals in order to inform, not to instruct. Giving the correct signals at the right time and in the right way is an essential part of good driving, as visible and audible signals are your only way of communicating with other road users. But it should always be borne in mind that you must never use signals to give orders to other drivers; a signal never gives you the right to make a move, such as a lane-change on a motorway, on the assumption that other drivers will give way. Police officers who deal with accidents are used to hearing the excuse, 'But I gave a signal', from the driver who has caused the trouble.

The art of proper signalling is a complex part of advanced driving which requires practice as well as learning. As in so many areas of advanced driving, the ground rules are simple: use only those signals described in the *Highway Code*. Do not make up your own signals or copy those adopted by other drivers; even if a personal signalling device seems perfectly clear to you, it could be dangerously misleading to someone who sees it for the first time and does not understand what you are trying to 'say'.

You must never expect other drivers to react in the right way to your correct signalling. Another motorist may not see your signal; he may not interpret it correctly; he may not act on it sensibly. Since you can never take it as read that another driver will recognise your intentions, always drive accordingly.

Direction indicators

Most of the signals you make during driving involve your car's direction indicators. They are used not only for turning left and right, but also for changing your position on the road. Use them thoughtfully and in good time so that other road users know what you are doing and can take action accordingly. For example, if you plan to turn right at a set of traffic lights, signal your intention early so that drivers behind you have plenty of time to move across to the inside lane and pass you on the nearside as you slow down. Keep your direction indicator winking all the time, even if your right-turning stream comes to a stop, so that other drivers behind you who want to go straight on do not get into the wrong lane.

When overtaking, keep the right-turn signal going until you begin to move back to the nearside, as its flashing will show oncoming drivers in the distance what you are doing. Although many motorists signal a left-turn as they move back in after an overtaking manoeuvre, this is generally unnecessary unless an unforeseen development ahead – something which should not happen with good planning – forces you to cut in sharply.

One of the most common driving faults you see in day-to-day motoring is failure to give proper signals. As an advanced driver, make sure that you are never guilty of this, as so many accidents are caused by sleepy or thoughtless drivers making manoeuvres without signalling. Always use your direction indicators properly at junctions, at roundabouts, when overtaking and when pulling in at the side of the road. Never think that a signal is unnecessary at quiet times of the day or night just because no-one else seems to be about. At the same time, signals are occasionally used over-zealously. When driving along an urban road dotted with parked cars, you do not need to signal every time you prepare to pass one; in a situation such as this, use your direction indicators intelligently when drivers behind would benefit from foreknowledge of an unexpected hazard, such as a particularly obstructive parked car or a cyclist on a relatively narrow road.

Hand signals

Hand signals are used far less frequently today than they used to be. However, there is still a place for them on occasions when they can emphasise your intentions in case

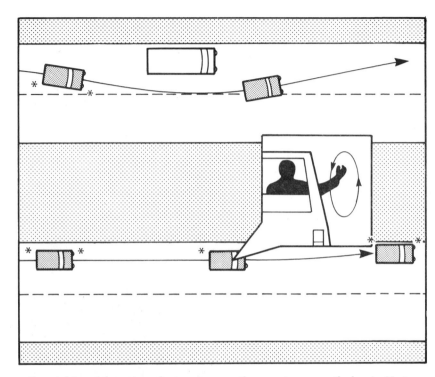

Overtaking (above) and stopping on the carriageway (below). Notice that when overtaking it is seldom necessary to signal left when moving back in front of the overtaken vehicle. When overtaking, you should be travelling in a straight line.

When stopping on the carriageway, a signal is enough where it is obvious that there is no left turn ahead. This will avoid confusing others, but the correct hand signal doesn't do any harm.

other drivers are in any doubt about what your direction indicators are being used for.

It used to be regarded as polite and normal to tell another driver of your intention to pull in at the side of the road by giving the left-turn hand signal – a circular wave of the hand in an anti-clockwise direction. Nowadays a simple left-turn signal on the direction indicator has become normal practice, but sometimes it is useful to wind down the window and give the old-fashioned hand signal as well. If a driver behind is particularly close or if traffic conditions seem to warrant it, use the hand signal to give more emphatic warning of your intentions. Just because you rarely see the signal used, do not ignore it altogether.

The same advice applies to the slowing-down signal – an up-and-down movement with the palm facing downwards, as if you are repeatedly pressing down on a weight. The right time for this signal is when you think that the driver behind is either too close or driving inattentively, and therefore might not realise that you are coming to a halt in traffic. The signal is particularly appropriate when you stop at a pedestrian crossing. Sometimes you see well-meaning drivers confuse the slowing-down and left-turn signals – a driver pulling in at the side of the road might give the 'I am stopping, you should too' up-and-down hand signal instead of the correct 'I am pulling into the kerb' rotary wave. He would be very surprised if you followed his instructions and pulled in behind to ask what the trouble was. Make sure, therefore, that you understand the distinction between these two hand signals so that you do not cause confusion on the occasions when their emphasis is valuable.

Left-turn and right-turn hand signals at junctions are also only necessary these days to emphasise your plans when you believe that other road users might benefit. A likely instance is when you plan to turn off where two side roads are close to each other, and you want to make it clear which one you are going to take. A right-turn hand signal can be valuable to show that you are intending to turn right and are not just pulling out to pass a parked vehicle. A left-turn hand signal can also help if you have to pull in to the side of the road at a point near a junction; ordinary use of the direction indicator alone might be interpreted as an intention to turn off down the side road. Remember also that hand signals can be useful to communicate your intentions to a police officer controlling traffic at a junction.

There are two hand signals which you must never use, although many drivers do in the belief that they are being courteous to other road users. These are the 'You can overtake me' wave to a following vehicle and the 'Please cross' gesture to pedestrians on a crossing. The problem with these is that if you make a mistake you could be guilty of causing an accident through your good intentions. Both

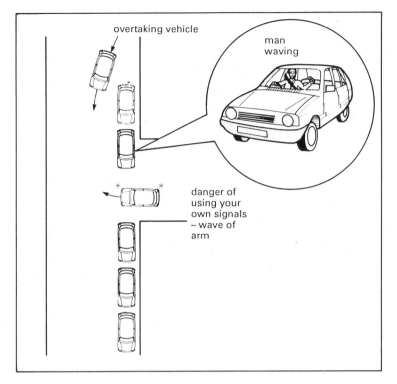

Danger of using a non-approved signal. You must never use a hand signal to indicate to a following vehicle 'you can overtake me'. If you make a mistake you could be guilty of causing an accident.

are omitted from the *Highway Code* because it is impossible for you to judge, from your position in the driving seat, whether other road-users – drivers or pedestrians – can safely accept your invitation. Leave it to them to make their own judgement. Since irresponsible drivers seem increasingly willing to break the law by overtaking on either side of traffic halted at a pedestrian crossing, the possible consequences of someone crossing at your request do not bear thinking about.

Headlight signals

There is also considerable risk of misunderstanding headlight signals, so use them only when they are valuable to draw the attention of other road users to your presence,

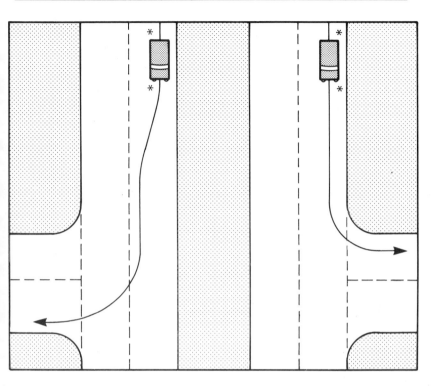

The lines to take when turning right or left. When turning left, avoid the unnecessary action of veering off to the right before negotiating the bend. Massive vehicles may have to do this (watch if you are driving behind one) but it is pointless and dangerous when driving a car. For the right turn, move over to the crown of the road in plenty of time, and be patient if the oncoming traffic is heavy.

as the *Highway Code* instructs. There are many circumstances where one driver uses a flash of the headlights to convey a message, and another driver interprets it as meaning something quite different. Most people have experienced examples of the confusion which can result. On a motorway, for example, a driver in lane 3 might flash his headlights as he comes up on a driver in lane 2 who is clearly looking for an opportunity to overtake: is he saying 'Look out, I'm coming through' or 'Come along, I'm easing off to let you out'?

The misused practice of headlamp flashing can just as easily cause trouble in town. If you are waiting to emerge from a side turning and an approaching car's headlights flash, do you take the message to be 'Don't move, I'm coming through' or 'Although I'm on the main road I'm slowing down to let you out'? More often than not 'flasher' and 'flashed-at' are on the same wavelength, but an accident is a real possibility every time they are not. You must, therefore, use headlight signals with great caution and only when it seems really necessary to warn other road users of your presence. Always be very careful to make sure that your intentions are not open to misinterpretation: although you will always use headlight flashing in accordance with the *Highway Code*, do not assume that other motorists will not read more into the message.

To add to the confusion, truck drivers have their own headlight code, whereby one driver tells another overtaking driver that the tail of his lorry has passed the front of his own and it is safe to pull back to the nearside. Since truck drivers are not used to cars being in this 'club', there is no need for you to adopt the same practice.

Brake lights

Brake lights cannot be misunderstood by anybody: they work automatically and their message is totally clear. The advanced driver, however, can also use his brake lights thoughtfully to convey additional information to following drivers. If you consider a driver is following too closely, it is a good idea when you approach any hazard to brake lightly at first to give him time to drop back to a safe distance before you have to brake more firmly. Never be self-righteous, though, in using brake lights to warn another driver to drop back. Some drivers have been known to be stupid enough to dab the brakes in a fast-moving flow of traffic just to shake someone off the back bumper; the result could be a chain reaction of braking which results in a nose-to-tail collision behind.

Thoughtful communication with your brake lights can be useful if you are the last car in a line of traffic stopped unexpectedly, perhaps just over the brow of a hill, round a bend or on a motorway. By applying the brakes regularly, even when stationary, your lights can warn the next driver that little bit earlier that traffic is at a standstill and not just moving slowly.

Remember that brake lights are just as likely as direction indicators to fail in one or both bulbs, so check all your lights regularly. An easy way to check is by running through the lights at night with your car positioned close to a wall or another vehicle: you should be able to see the glow from each bulb quite clearly.

Horn

As with the headlights, the horn should be used only to inform other road users of your presence. Remember that it is illegal, except in an emergency to avoid an accident, to sound your horn between 11.30pm and 7.00am in a built-up area or at any time of day or night if the car is stationary.

Sensible use of the horn is valuable as a warning. If children are playing in a residential street, or an absent-minded driver starts to pull out from a side road in front of you, a polite tap on the button might be useful. Never use the horn, though, as a substitute for the observation, planning and courtesy which are the mark of a good driver. Several slightly longer notes on the horn can often be a good idea on a main road when overtaking a driver who may not be aware of your presence. A lorry or tractor driver in a noisy cab, for example, may have such restricted rearward vision that he has not noticed you. Always remember, however, that British drivers seem far more ready to take offence at the sound of a horn than their continental counterparts, so use your horn with discretion when overtaking. If they think a note on the horn is not delivered politely, some drivers take it as a reprimand, a challenge or an insult, and react accordingly.

Thoughtful and courteous use of the horn is what counts. You may not use it often, but to believe that it should never be used is a mistake.

Summary

- Use your *direction indicators* to inform other drivers of your intentions, not to give orders to them. Use them correctly, consistently and thoughtfully.

- Use only the *hand signals* given in the *Highway Code*: although you see hand signals given relatively rarely these days, they should still be employed in circumstances where other road users would benefit from emphasis of your intentions.
- Remember that *headlight signals* can easily be misunderstood by other road users; flash your lights only when it is necessary to warn other road users of your presence and when your intentions cannot be misinterpreted.
- Use the *horn* sensibly in the same way as headlight signals: to let other road users know you are there.

12

DRIVING AT NIGHT

Night driving is an essential part of motoring for most people, so if you have just passed your test do not keep putting off the day when you first drive in darkness. Like all other aspects of handling a car safely, night driving presents no undue risks as long as you observe the rules. Indeed, there are positive advantages to driving at night, when traffic begins to thin out: the experience can be less stressful and your journey time can be reduced. Driving in the dark, however, can be dangerous if you do not obey the rules, especially on a long run when you are feeling tired. Always remember the extra dangers of allowing your concentration to lapse, because accident rates per vehicle mile do rise dramatically at night.

Lighting equipment

All the lights on your car should be in working order, with headlights operative on both dipped and main beams. If you are in any doubt about the beam alignment, have it checked at a garage which has the appropriate equipment. If you are planning a long night journey with a heavy load weighing down the back of your car, it can be wise to have the headlights adjusted temporarily, but remember to have them returned to the usual setting after the journey. Having the nose of your car pointing up a few degrees can be enough for your dipped beam to dazzle oncoming drivers, and for your main beam uselessly to illuminate the tops of the hedgerows. Before having any adjustment made, though, check in the manufacturer's handbook to see whether your car has a simple device to allow you to change the headlight angle yourself.

Be seen at night. Many drivers are content with using their sidelights in a built-up area after dark (left) but as the picture (right) so clearly shows, dipped beams are preferable. They not only increase your own vision ahead, for some street lighting is less than ideal, but – more importantly – they allow you to be seen better by other road users.

Regular checking

Check regularly that all your lights work. You can check most of them yourself, but you will need someone else to watch your brake lights while you press the pedal. If no-one else is available, simply park your car close to a wall and watch for the reflected glow as you try the brakes. While driving, you can check the lights from time to time in a stationary line of traffic by looking for the reflections in the bodywork of cars ahead and behind.

Auxiliary lights

Most modern cars are equipped with excellent headlights of the quartz-halogen variety but if you own an older car, and are unhappy with the lights, investigate the possibility of changing them. Fitting auxiliary lights is always a good idea, but if you do this without changing poor headlights you might find the contrast between brilliant auxiliary beam and feeble dipped beam all the more disconcerting. Quartz-halogen lights give a much more powerful and whiter beam. Auxiliary fog and spot lights are valuable aids to driving safely at night, but make sure you have the beam adjusted properly. The law requires that auxiliary

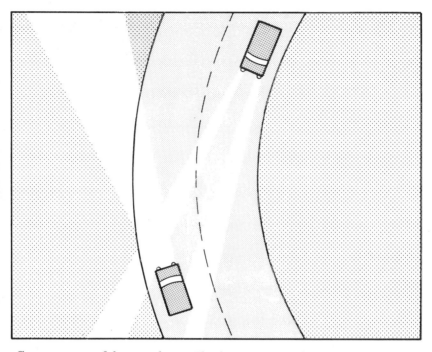

Courteous use of the main beam. The driver on the left doesn't need to dip his lights in this situation, because his beam will not strike the oncoming car. The driver on the right should dip his lights to avoid dazzling the first driver.

lights must be fitted in pairs, because a single beam could be mistaken for a motorcycle, and they must be mounted within the dimensions laid down by the Department of the Environment. The law also states that very low-slung lights may only be used in conditions of fog or falling snow.

Reversing and hazard lights
Most cars are also equipped with reversing lights, which are tremendously valuable in illuminating obstacles and pedestrians when you reverse your car. If your car does not have them fitted, buy a pair at an accessory shop and have them wired to come on automatically when reverse gear is selected. Extra brake lights for installation in the rear window can also be bought at accessory shops. They

are not really necessary in view of the intensity of the brake lights now fitted to modern cars, but they do offer one advantage: their high location allows drivers several cars back in a stream of traffic to have earlier warning when you brake. A few new cars are now sold in Britain with a high-level central brake light fitted at the base of the rear window. Some drivers find this type of auxiliary brake light distracting because it is at eye level, but it can also provide earlier warning when you spot it in the distance through the windows of cars ahead. All modern cars have hazard warning lights operated by a switch which enables all four direction indicators to flash simultaneously as warning when you have to stop at an awkward spot in an emergency, such as on a motorway hard shoulder. A good accessory shop can supply the necessary modification if your car does not have hazard lights.

Yellow lights
Never fit yellow bulbs or lens covers, or any substance to colour the glass, to your headlights except when driving in France. French-registered cars must be fitted with yellow lights in the interests of reducing dazzle, but this is achieved only because partially opaque colouring reduces the total light output. Other European countries do not favour yellow headlights, and neither should you.

Eyesight

It is just as important to make sure that the driver, as well as the car, is properly prepared for night driving. The dangers of wearing 'night driving' glasses, or just ordinary sunglasses, were discussed in Chapter 8. Any spectacles which reduce dazzle are not a good idea because they cut down the total light reaching your eyes, making dimly-lit hazards – pedestrians or parked cars in shadows, for example – harder to see. Since any sight deficiencies are relatively worse at night, make sure your eyes are checked regularly by an optician. Should you be in any doubt about your vision being worse in darkness than during the day, have your eyes tested for night driving purposes; an optician will be able to prescribe spectacles accordingly if you need them.

Fatigue

Few people regularly drive long distances at night, so on the rare occasions when this is necessary do not underestimate the need to prepare yourself properly. What could otherwise be an enjoyable drive over near-deserted roads could turn into a worrying struggle to stay awake at the wheel. Many accidents are caused by drivers falling asleep, so be very conscious of the fact that it is all too easy to become overwhelmed by fatigue without being aware of it. Do not embark on a long night drive after a strenuous day, and before you set out avoid eating a heavy meal, which might make you feel drowsy. Certainly keep off all alcohol as your judgement and concentration deteriorate after just one drink. Never take pills to stay awake, since such drugs can have dangerous side-effects which affect your ability at the wheel.

Refresher breaks
Keep asking yourself throughout your journey whether you feel at all tired, and stop for a break if you do. Remember that bitter experience has led to 'Tiredness can kill' signs being erected on routes where many holidaymakers drive through the night. However good you feel, do not drive for more than two hours, at the very most, without a break to stretch your legs, breathe fresh air and, perhaps, have a cup of coffee. The dangers of tiredness become more acute in the later stages of a journey, so if you start to feel sleepy stop the car somewhere safe (never on a motorway hard shoulder) for a quick nap; dozing for a short time can make you feel quite revived. Another good idea is to go for a short but vigorous run up the road to get your circulation going again.

Air circulation
Although you should never reach a state where such extreme measures to keep yourself awake become necessary, always err well on the side of caution. Fatigue at the wheel can be as lethal as driving under the influence of drink or drugs. One precaution you can take is to turn the heater down when you feel tired, as a warm fug is just the atmosphere to make your eyes feel heavy. Keep plenty

of fresh, cool air blowing through the vents and open a window; having diagonally opposite windows open will allow an invigorating rush of air through the car.

Dazzle and visibility

Novice drivers invariably find that their biggest worry about night driving is glare from the headlights of oncoming vehicles, which we have already talked about in Chapter 8. Almost all drivers find that their eyes at first are drawn involuntarily towards approaching headlights, but in time they learn to make a conscious effort to look away and concentrate the gaze on the road directly ahead. With experience this reaction becomes second nature, and you start to appreciate oncoming headlights for the extra light which they throw into your path.

Occasionally you will meet another motorist who is too inconsiderate or forgetful to dip his headlights when you approach. You should always dip your lights when you see the cast of a beam approaching, and certainly before the other vehicle is in sight. If the other driver does not respond to your dipping action, it is acceptable to use a quick flash on to main beam to remind him. Invariably this will bring the desired relief to your eyes as the other driver reacts, but occasionally he will stay on main beam (or perhaps what appears to be main beam, because his dipped headlights are way out of adjustment or his vehicle is heavily laden). You may be tempted to retaliate by staying on main beam yourself, but this response is foolish; it means that there are two dazzled drivers on the road instead of one, which in turn doubles the danger. Furthermore, remember how the human eye works: while it can quickly contract the pupil to shut out unwanted light, it takes much longer to dilate afterwards. For several risky seconds after your two vehicles have passed, both of you will be driving in a semi-dazzled state.

It is essential to remember the basic rule of good driving – always drive at a speed which enables you to stop within the distance you can see – when you are motoring at night. This means keeping your speed down so that you can always pull up within the distance illuminated by your headlights. On dipped beam along a straight road this may mean that your speed has to be lower at night than during the day. Keep your headlights on main beam on country roads except when other road users approach; as well as car and lorry drivers, this means motorcyclists, cyclists and pedestrians. You should keep the vehicle ahead at such a distance that it is in the far fringe of light from your dipped beam, remembering that you must also maintain a safe stopping distance. When changing from main to dipped beam, reduce your speed if necessary to a level appropriate to your shorter range of visibility.

Two points of advice are worthwhile for the use of dipped and main beam headlights when driving round bends. On a left-hander, make sure that you dip early to avoid your main beam dazzling the oncoming driver as it sweeps across the inside of the curve. Conversely, on a right-hander you do not need to dip quite so early, and strictly you may not need to dip at all as your headlights shine towards the outer edge of the curve. Since approaching drivers may not be aware of this and will be waiting for you to dip your headlights, it is generally courteous to do so even though it may not really be necessary.

Always drive on dipped lights when following another driver so that you do not dazzle him in his mirrors. You should also use dipped lights when following motorcyclists or cyclists as a rider can find his visibility impaired when his own shadow is thrown forward by main beam lights. If a driver behind is thoughtless enough to keep his lights on main beam, raise your hand to the mirror to show him that he is distracting you. If he does not respond, use the dip facility on your mirror or move it by a few degrees so that his lights can still be seen but do not dazzle you. Either way, remember to return the mirror to its usual position as soon as the offending lights have gone.

Use dipped lights, rather than sidelights (or parking lights, as they are perhaps more aptly described), when driving in town, on illuminated motorways and in bad weather. Although new cars are now fitted with 'dim-dip' lights, which give an intensity halfway between sidelights and dipped lights, it is still best to use dipped lights at all times when it is dark.

Never hesitate to switch on your sidelights as soon as

daylight begins to fade, and use your headlights as soon as you consider them necessary. Even though the light at dawn and dusk can be good enough for you to see quite happily without headlights, remember that the point of using lights in fading light is for you to be seen by other road users. Many drivers with a frugal nature seem to think that headlights should be saved until they are necessary to see by, and may give you a reproving 'flash' when you have switched yours on good and early. Their sense of economy is misplaced for two reasons: it costs nothing to run a car's headlights since battery life is not shortened, and a semi-invisible car is a very dangerous object.

To make the most of the illumination be sure to keep your headlights clean; even a thin film of grime can cut the light output by half, while only a tenth of the light may get through a thick layer. If your car's bodywork is at all dirty, you can be sure that your lights are not as bright as they could be. On damp winter roads it is surprising how quickly mud can coat your lights; just think how often you need to use windscreen wipers and washers to clear your view, and then imagine the layer of dirt your headlights are trying to pierce. If conditions are particularly mucky, therefore, stop every now and then to wipe down the lights. It is a good idea to keep tissue in the car for this purpose and soak it in washer fluid so that all the dirt comes off, unless you are lucky enough to own a car with headlight washers and wipers.

Summary

- Always be sure that all your *lights are working*, and that your headlights are correctly adjusted.
- Stop for *regular breaks* when making a long journey at night. *Fatigue* is very dangerous: when you begin to feel slightly tired your concentration and speed of reaction suffer; sleepiness makes you lethal.
- Use *dipped* and *main beam* headlights intelligently, and make sure that you can always stop safely in the distance illuminated by your dipped lights.
- Do not delay in switching on your headlights in *fading light* or *bad weather*. Make sure that your headlights are always kept clean.

13

TYRES

Considering the importance of tyres from the safety point of view, it is surprising that so many motorists seem to take them more or less for granted. Many drivers fail to check their tyres often enough for pressure, damage or wear. Although tyres have been developed by manufacturers to the point where they offer remarkable levels of grip on dry and wet roads and are extremely resistant to punctures, their qualities are compromised if they are under-inflated, badly worn or damaged. As these four footprints of tread are your only contact with the road, it is vital for everyone's safety that your tyres are in good condition.

Tyre technicalities

All new cars are equipped with radial-ply tyres, although cross-ply tyres were once usual. Apart from classic cars, a small proportion of older cars on the roads today are still running on cross-ply tyres: if yours is one of these, it would be well worth fitting radials, which offer superior roadholding and handling qualities. Remember, however, that it is illegal to mix tyres. All your tyres (including the spare) should be radials or cross-plies, although the legal requirement is not quite so inflexible. Another option is remould tyres, but these are best avoided despite their appeal from the cost point of view. Tyres are so imporant for the safety of everyone on the road that too much economy is foolish.

Most motorists replace their tyres with new ones of identical make and type. This is by far the best course, but if you decide to upgrade your tyres perhaps in the interests of better grip or longer life, check with a tyre specialist or a dealer familiar with your make of car whether this is wise. Manufacturers invariably fit the tyres most suitable for the car, so you may find that giving in to a desire to fit larger tyres (and perhaps wheels) results in unacceptably heavy steering, more road noise and an inferior ride. If the tyres are too wide they can even rub on the bodywork when the car is driven round a corner or over a bump. Grip may be better, but ask yourself whether you really need it. While economy in tyres is not to be recommended, do not allow yourself to be browbeaten by a tyre specialist into buying better tyres than your car or style of motoring require.

Do pay the extra charge to have your wheels balanced when new tyres are fitted. Out-of-balance wheels can cause vibrations which become progressively more unpleasant – and wearing for the occupants of the car – as speed increases, especially when fitted to the front wheels. It is also sensible to run-in new tyres by driving more gently for the first 100 miles or so, as the tread needs to be 'scrubbed' before it will grip with maximum efficiency.

A few words about the coded markings on tyres are also worth while, as many motorists, not surprisingly, are baffled by the strings of numerals and letters used by manufacturers. A typical notation might be 165/70 SR 14. The figures refer to the size, which in this case means a tyre width of 165mm with a 'low profile' shoulder (the area between wheel rim and circumference) 70 per cent of the normal size to fit a 14-inch wheel. Quite why metric and imperial measurements are still mixed is a source of mystery. The letters refer to one of three codes denoting the maximum speed permissible on the tyre: SR tyres are for cars capable of up to 113mph, HR for 113mph–130mph and VR for over 130mph. Although these speed bands are quite academic for British motoring, you should stick with the type which the manufacturer specifies for your car.

Looking after your tyres

Careless driving can damage your car's tyres all too easily. Driving over a kerb or scraping the edge of a tyre against a kerb can cause damage which might have a disastrous result – sudden deflation – if you do not have the tyre checked. Look for splits or bulges in the tyre wall as obvious signs, but serious internal damage does not always show on the outside. As far as tyres are concerned, it is

This photograph shows the distortion that a tyre is subjected to when the car is cornered at full lock at 25mph. This sort of treatment will wear your tyres out very quickly. PHOTO COURTESY OF SP TYRES UK LIMITED

much better to be safe than sorry; have your tyres checked if you believe you might have damaged them.

Locking the wheels when braking, spinning the driving wheels under harsh acceleration and quick cornering will all wear out the tyres more quickly. Since tyres are an appreciable part of the cost you incur in running a car, it is logical to look after them properly by driving with care and keeping them at the right pressure.

Tyre pressure
Follow the manufacturer's recommended pressures (remembering that a slightly higher pressure is generally suggested for sustained motorway cruising or carrying a heavy load): do not experiment with pressures, as you are unlikely to improve on the manufacturer's findings and may well instead land yourself in trouble in an emergency. Pressure checks should be carried out at the start of a trip when the air in the tyres is cold; pressure readings are higher when the air inside a tyre has warmed up.

Four examples of abnormal tyre wear caused through neglect. Periodic examination of your tyres can spot trouble early enough to prevent it becoming a problem.

a)   *Centre tread wear as a result of overinflation.*

b)   *Sidewall bulge caused by impact damage.*

c)   *Shoulder wear caused by incorrect tracking.*

d)   *Bald spot caused by faulty shock absorbers.*

e)   *Steel wire exposed on shoulder as a result of incorrect tracking.*

PHOTOS COURTESY OF GOODYEAR GREAT BRITAIN LIMITED

Recommended pressures naturally allow for this, so you will end up under-inflating your tyres if you check them when warm. Since garage pressure gauges can vary, it is a good idea, for the sake of consistency, to use a good quality pocket pressure gauge which can be bought from an accessory shop.

Aquaplaning on poor tyres. A badly worn tyre can displace so little water that it skates over the surface without even touching the road. If you are driving too fast, even a perfectly sound tyre can aquaplane. Needless to say, this is extremely dangerous.

It is inadvisable to lower tyre pressures to cope with mud or snow; you will not necessarily have better grip, and you could damage the tyres by running them under-inflated. Should you forget what you have done, you could come a cropper on a bend because of the poor roadholding which results when the tyres squirm under cornering forces. Some motorists raise pressures to achieve a slight improvement in fuel economy, but the penalty is poorer grip, especially on wet roads.

Over-inflated and under-inflated tyres can also wear unevenly across their widths. If you notice uneven wear, make sure that the tyres have not been inflated wrongly, perhaps due to a faulty gauge. Failing this, the steering or suspension will be out of alignment, possibly because you have run over a kerb or a severe pothole. If this is the case, have the alignment corrected by a garage.

Replacing worn tyres
The law requires that tyres should be replaced when the tread depth over three-quarters of a tyre's width has worn down to its last millimetre. This is remarkably lenient as a tyre's grip will have deteriorated considerably by this point, so you would be well advised to consider replacement when the tread depth is around 3mm. A simple gauge is available to measure this accurately. Unless you have a four-wheel drive car, it is a good idea to swap your tyres between front and back wheels about halfway through their life, as tyres on the driven wheels generally wear out more quickly.

The real danger of worn tyres occurs in wet weather, for the tiny depth of tread is simply unable to cope with its task of squeezing up water from the road. For a tyre to bite down on to the road at 60mph, several gallons of water must be cleared every second; a tyre clearly does this job more efficiently the newer it is. If you are particularly sensitive to your car's handling, you will feel worn tyres offering less grip in wet weather long before the 1mm limit is reached. The first time you notice this is obviously the moment to fit one or more new tyres.

A very worn or totally bald tyre can shift so little water that it quickly rides up on to the surface, skating along on a film of water without touching the road at all. The dangers of this condition – known as aquaplaning – are self-evident: steering control, sideways grips and braking are all completely lost. Even a pefectly sound tyre can aquaplane if you drive fast over a deep puddle. If you have done this, it is quite likely that you have experienced the feeling of the steering becoming momentarily light and lifeless in your hands.

Punctures
As well as giving less grip on a wet road, worn tyres are also more susceptible to punctures. All tyres, of course, can puncture, but sudden deflation is mercifully rare these

days. Many drivers neglect to carry a good spare tyre or to check its pressure along with the other four, but all eventually come to regret their haste when a puncture occurs, perhaps far from home on a wet night. Even driving just a short distance on a flat tyre can ruin it. When you suffer a puncture, have the tyre repaired (if this is possible) or replaced as soon as possible, since it is illegal and foolish to continue to drive around with a useless spare tyre.

Many motorists worry about how they would cope if they are unlucky enough to suffer a tyre blow-out when travelling quickly. It requires considerable presence of mind in the eventuality, but you should brake very gently and try to steer straight ahead – or slightly to the left if you are in danger of involving following vehicles – until you come to a stop. Even with a front wheel puncture, some steering is maintained as long as the deflated tyre is not rolled off the rim by violent movement of the wheel. Such accidents usually result from lack of attention to tyres: heavy braking or swerving after a puncture, overloading the tyres, running them in damaged condition or fitting tyres of the wrong type can all be contributory factors. Insufficient pressure causes many motorway accidents, because a tyre flexes too much, heats up and finally fails when the rubber melts and the tread peels away from the casing.

Summary

- When buying *new tyres*, always make sure that you select a make and type suitable for your car, preferably by matching the existing tyres; radials and cross-plies should not be mixed.
- Keep a regular eye on *tyre condition* by checking pressures and making sure no damage has occurred. Have your tyres checked by a specialist if you ever have cause to believe that you might have damaged them.
- A car is extremely dangerous on *worn tyres*, especially in wet weather, because grip is greatly reduced.

14

OVERTAKING

Every aspect of overtaking is related to one of the basic rules of safe driving and therefore discussed in other chapters of this book. There are some specific points about overtaking, however, which you should always bear in mind.

Why and when?

The first question you should ask yourself, whenever you consider overtaking, is whether the manoeuvre is strictly necessary. If you wish to pass a slow-moving vehicle which is genuinely impeding your progress, and can do so safely, then by all means overtake. Very often, however, overtaking is pointless if it serves only to move you up one place in a line of traffic. Do not let an instinctive desire to get ahead encourage you to overtake; your manoeuvre should be motivated only by the practical consideration of improving your progress during a journey.

The second question – *when* to overtake – is even more important. On an ordinary road, overtaking means that you must spend time on the wrong side of the road, which is an exceedingly dangerous place to be. Careful planning, rapid thinking and decisiveness are all essential. You must be certain that the road is clear far enough ahead to allow you to pull out, accelerate, overtake and pull back in again without alarming an oncoming driver in the distance or causing the driver you are passing to take action to help you out of a sticky situation. Overtaking can take a considerable time, even if you use all the acceleration available to you. If an approaching vehicle comes into sight over a brow or round a bend while you are still making your manoeuvre, you could be in trouble – and you will scare the drivers around you.

Be aware of the relative speeds involved. If you overtake at a speed of 60mph and the vehicle you are passing is doing 40mph, you haul it in at only 20mph. If an oncoming vehicle is travelling at 60mph, the rate at which the two of you close is 120mph (60mph + 60mph), a speed at which a long gap shortens *very* quickly. You do not have to be good at arithmetic to understand that a dangerous situation can develop rapidly if you make a mistake in your timing. You *cannot* make mistakes when you overtake.

Besides assessing whether there is time to overtake safely, the operation must be planned with great care, not with the air of optimism which a few irresponsible drivers employ. As well as allowing for oncoming vehicles, you must be prepared for the driver who might come out of a side turning, drive or lay-by. He may pause at the main road, look to his right to check that nothing is coming on his side of the road and then pull out; it might never occur to him that an overtaking car could be approaching from the left. Since this terrifying scenario happens with appalling frequency, you should never overtake when you can see a side road ahead, even if there is no vehicle visible when you are considering the manoeuvre. It is impossible to allow for a concealed drive or lane which has no signpost, but always be prepared for the possibility and be ready to sound the horn and/or flash the headlights to draw attention to yourself if a vehicle does appear from 'nowhere'.

Overtaking procedure

After checking the *why* and *when* of overtaking, you should turn your attention to *how* you will carry out the manoeuvre. Once you have satisfied yourself that there is plenty of room for you to overtake safely, you should check your mirror before starting to move out. You must not be so close to the vehicle ahead that you need to move just to see whether the road is clear, and you must be certain when planning to overtake that there is a suitable gap ahead for you to pull in again safely. You should be especially aware of this point if the vehicle in front is a large lorry which conceals the traffic directly ahead of it; it is quite common for a driver to embark on a manoeuvre only to find that he has to pass two or three lorries in one go, not one.

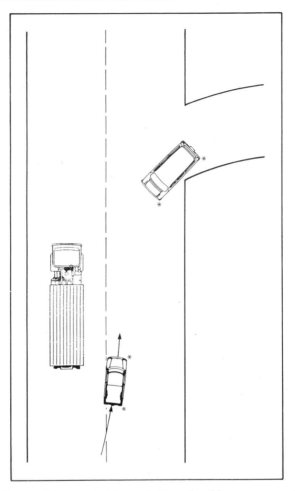

Dangers of overtaking at a side road. You should never overtake when you can see a side road or lay-by ahead, even if no vehicle is visible.

If there is no-one behind you who is about to overtake and no-one already coming up on the outside (and possibly briefly out of your view in the mirrors), give a right-turn signal, change down to a lower gear for stronger acceleration if necessary, and press the throttle firmly but smoothly as you move out. The gear you choose should be able to get you through to the completion of the manoeuvre before the engine revs reach the point where you need to change up. This will enable you to keep both hands on the wheel throughout the exercise.

As your car draws level with the rear of the vehicle you are about to pass, keep a careful eye out for any signs that the other driver might change course, perhaps by overtaking the vehicle in front of him or turning right. It is more than a slim possibility that he will do either without checking in his mirror or signalling. If he starts to move, or even if you suspect that he might, give one or more sharp blasts of the horn to warn him of your presence. This practice is used frequently on the continent, and ought to be used more willingly by drivers in Britain.

Some people seem to resent being overtaken and behave quite insanely. They may even close the gap ahead of them to shut you out in the right-hand lane or accelerate while you are passing. Always keep your temper under control and resist any urge to retaliate, either by trying to race the driver or carving your way into the shrinking gap ahead of him; two angry drivers are twice as dangerous as one. Treat such stupid behaviour in the only sensible way, by pulling back into place behind the vehicle.

Thankfully, the other driver will almost always let you through, so it is then up to you not to cut back in front of him. As soon as the vehicle appears in your mirror, it is safe for you to return to the correct side of the road.

Summary

- *Why?* Always ask yourself whether an overtaking manoeuvre is really *necessary.*
- *When?* Ensure that you always overtake *safely*, when there is plenty of time available to complete the manoeuvre. Do not overtake if you would have to pass a *side turning* while doing so, even if no vehicles are waiting to pull out on to your road.
- *How?* Check your mirror and signal before moving out; engage a lower gear if necessary and accelerate firmly but smoothly; do not cut in sharply at the end of the manoeuvre; be prepared for foolish behaviour from the driver you are passing.

DRIVING IN WINTER

Although British winters are mild for most of the time, a cold snap always makes roads treacherous and catches many motorists by surprise. It is important that a driver knows how to cope in conditions of sleet, snow and ice, and that his car is in good shape and able to deal with the demands imposed on it. Learn with experience how to drive safely in ice and snow: some people are timid and abandon their cars before they need to, while others do not make proper allowances for the conditions and end up causing accidents.

Winter equipment

Tyre grip is your first priority in winter, so make sure that all your tyres (including the spare) are in good condition and have plenty of tread.

Improving tyre grip
The best policy for motorists who are unable to leave their cars in the garage when it snows is to carry a set of chains or straps which can be fitted to the ordinary tyres when the going gets tough. Modern grip improvers can be fitted far more quickly than old-fashioned chains, but practise their use at home before you have to do it in a blizzard.

All forms of grip improvers are designed to work when there is a layer of snow between the tyres and the road surface, so take them off as soon as you are on a clear road again. The raised sections which dig down into snow also prevent the tyres from gripping well in normal conditions. You will quickly wear out straps or chains on normal roads, and the car will be uncomfortable to ride in. A worn chain can be hazardous if it snaps, for a piece of flying metal could hurt a passer-by or damage your car's bodywork. If you feel that your driving needs make it worthwhile, a set of knobbly-treaded 'mud and snow' or 'town and country' tyres might be the best answer; they deal with mud and fresh snow quite well, but remember that their grip in normal conditions is not so good.

Necessary additions

A vital piece of winter equipment is a small shovel kept in the boot. Apart from clearing away snow, it could be useful for gathering roadside grit to spread under the driving wheels if you run out of grip on a hill. Another idea for getting moving again if the driving wheels spin uselessly on ice or snow is to carry a couple of sacks and some tough string to tie them to the doorhandles. You can put them under the wheels for grip, and once you are rolling keep pressing on until a level road is reached before stopping to retrieve your sacks; but make sure that you use enough string to allow the sacks to trail clear of the back wheels.

Visibility aids

Visibility is important, so make sure that your windscreen wiper blades and washers are in good order. Add a 'screen-wash' fluid to the water in your washer bottle to give a better cleaning solution which will not freeze, and ensure that all the car's lights are kept as clean as the windows. The heated rear window fitted to most cars is invaluable, so buy a demisting element from an accessory shop if your car does not have one. Keep an aerosol de-icer and a plastic scraper in the car to clear frost from all the windows; another piece of sacking is also useful to drape over the windscreen if you have to leave the car for a few hours in freezing temperatures.

Condensation control

So many modern cars have complex heating and ventilation systems that it is worth studying the manufacturer's handbook to learn how to make the most of the controls. It is easy to obtain lots of heat to keep you warm, but make sure that you know the best combination of settings to keep all the windows free of condensation.

On a cold or wet day you often see cars with some of the side windows misted up, which makes you wonder how a driver manages to see properly at junctions; even worse, a few drivers even make do with wiping a smeary gap so they can see through the windscreen. Unless your car's heating system is unable to work efficiently, perhaps because air inlets are blocked with autumn leaves, it should be able to keep condensation off all windows. Condensation accumulates more quickly if you have several passengers in the car, so it may occasionally be necessary to open the windows a little – just half an inch should do – to keep plenty of fresh air circulating. Remember that it is just as dangerous to allow the interior to get so stuffy that there is a possibility of the driver drifting off to sleep.

Driving in fog
The basic lighting needs for your car for night driving are covered in Chapter 12, but it is worth adding that auxiliary lighting is even more valuable in winter. Since modern cars generally have very good quartz–halogen headlights, the most useful additional lighting is a pair of fog lamps. Check with a dealer specialising in your make of car what the manufacturer recommends.

One very valuable option, high-intensity rear lighting for use in fog (sometimes a single lamp, sometimes a pair), is fitted to most cars these days, but if your car lacks these it would be a very good idea to invest in a pair. These lights penetrate much further through fog than ordinary rear lights, so they give following drivers earlier warning of your presence. Since so many cars now have these lights, it is worth pointing out that in heavy traffic in fog, especially on a busy motorway or dual carriageway, a car without them becomes harder to spot among all the bright red beacons.

A word of advice, however, because the use of these lights is greatly abused. Many drivers switch on their high-intensity rear lights long before they are necessary, perhaps in moderate rain or slight mist. Worse still, a few drivers are absent-minded enough to forget to switch them off again, sometimes for days. The dazzle these lamps cause when visibility remains reasonably good is very

One method of getting traction on snow or ice is to tie sacks to the door handles of your car, and then drive over the sacks, having ensured that the rope is long enough to let the sacks trail free of the car once you have got going. This way you will not have to stop to retrieve the sacks until you have reached firmer ground.

irritating and tiring for drivers behind. Furthermore, it is possible that a pair which suddenly appears in the distance can be mistaken for brake lights. In short, use them when visibility drops below 100 metres, and do not forget to switch them off again when the weather improves.

Problems of freezing
A few other points about looking after your car are worth mentioning before we turn to the techniques of driving on slippery roads. As winter approaches, you should make sure that your engine's cooling system is topped up with a water/anti-freeze mixture. A lock which has frozen up can be thawed with a key heated by a match. Salt is very good

at thawing snow and ice on the road, but it can also attack your car's bodywork; hose down the underside regularly through the winter, and especially thoroughly when spring comes.

Skidding

The golden rule when driving on a slippery road surface is to do everything as smoothly and gently as possible: this is good advice for driving in all conditions, but it becomes absolutely vital when there is snow or ice on the road. You must constantly be aware of the danger of skidding because the grip from your car's tyres is greatly reduced.

A skid is invariably provoked by harsh movement with the steering wheel or using the brake or accelerator pedals too insensitively. When the road is slippery you should make each steering movement extremely gently, especially on snow or ice, and apply the same light touch to the brake and accelerator pedals. Skids usually involve either the front or rear tyres losing their grip, but sometimes all four wheels can end up sliding. Whether the front or rear wheels cease to grip depends on a car's handling characteristics and how it is driven, but generally rear-wheel drive cars are more likely to slide at the rear and front-wheel drive cars are more likely to lose grip at the front. The most common reasons are cornering too fast, applying too much power and braking on a bend. The feeling of a car beginning to move sideways can be unnerving, but the worry of skidding is greatly reduced if you know what to do.

There are many theories about how to deal with a skid, but the only correct method is the one practised by experts such as traffic police and experienced racing drivers. First, do not panic and stand on the brakes in an attempt to stop the car, as this will send the car even further out of control; stay right away from the brake pedal.

A rear-wheel skid is most commonly caused by applying too much power when driving a rear-wheel drive car through a corner. If this happens, the correct procedure is to lift off the accelerator to remove the

A special tyre for special conditions. The Avon 'Turbospeed CR28' incorporates widely-spaced ribs and bold open blocks for extra grip in wet, slippery conditions. The blocks expel water and slush from the contact patch for undiminished bite on soaking roads. PHOTO COURTESY OF AVON RUBBER PLC

slide-provoking power from the wheels, and steer into the skid so that the front wheels remain pointing in the direction you wish to travel. On a right-hand bend with the tail of the car swinging out to the left, therefore, you have to steer to the left to keep the wheels pointing down the path of the road. This opposite-lock, as it is called, will pull the car back into line, but take care not to hold the opposite-lock for a moment longer than necessary as the tail will swing out the other way. Pay off the steering as the car corrects its course so that you are ready to resume steering round the bend again. If you are too slow to correct the steering, the tail can start to act like a pendulum, swinging first one way and then the other, forcing you to apply opposite-lock in the other direction.

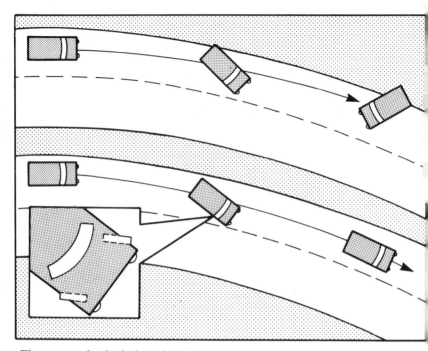

The rear wheel skid and its cure. In the top example, the skid is uncorrected, and the inevitable spin occurs. The competent driver will steer in the same direction as the rear swing (bottom) and thus cancel it. The manoeuvre calls for neat judgement with the steering wheel, or an even worse opposite skid can result.

You must also avoid over-correcting the steering, as this can also induce a pendulum effect. All of this requires skill and sensitivity, but attempting to control a skidding car is better than doing nothing at all. If left unchecked, the car will skid off the road completely, or, equally seriously, collide with another vehicle.

Front-wheel skids are more likely to occur in a front-wheel drive car as a result of applying too much power, steering too sharply or braking too heavily, but steering and braking mistakes can also cause a rear-wheel drive car to skid in this way. Front-wheel skids can be more difficult to deal with because the car simply ploughs on in a straight line when it should be turning or stopping. If the

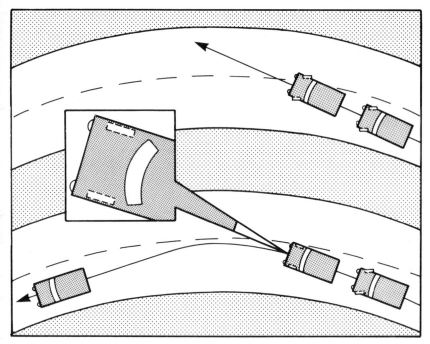

The front wheel skid and its cure. Uncorrected, this skid will take you away from the curve you wish to follow, with potentially disastrous results. The solution to the problem is to steer into the skid, feet away from the pedals, to enable the front tyres to resume their traction. Once this has happened, further attempts can be made to steer your desired course, though fine judgement is needed at the wheel. Over-correction can lead to a pendulum-swinging effect on the rear of the car, which can be just as dangerous as the original skid. Most front-wheel skids are caused by lack of judgement on the part of the driver, though sometimes one can be forced on you by circumstances, so it's vital that you know how to cope.

cause is over-heavy braking which robs you of steering control, the answer is to release the brake pedal momentarily to allow the front wheels to turn again, and then re-apply the brakes more gently. The most effective way of stopping quickly is by using 'cadence' braking – the on-off braking technique outlined in Chapter 6. If you have tried to put too much power through the front wheels, lifting off the accelerator will allow the front wheels to grip

– and steer – again. If the front-wheel skid is provoked by turning the steering wheel too sharply, your corrective action must also be to the steering. Straighten the wheel towards the straight-ahead position until you feel the tyres regain their grip, then start steering again, more gently this time, in the required direction, using all your judgement to avoid provoking another skid.

While all this advice ought to enable you to deal with a skidding car, great presence of mind is necessary when you have to put it into practice. A skid can occur so quickly and unexpectedly that you are best equipped to react if your actions are almost instinctive. This skill comes to some drivers more naturally than others, but all benefit from practising it. Since there is no substitute for acquiring experience in controlling a skidding car, it is very worthwhile to refine these instinctive reactions by practising on a skid pan. With an expert instructor by your side, you can learn so much in an hour or two that you will be able to control your car with far greater competence and confidence. You will find out exactly how skids are provoked, what they feel like and how you should deal with them, to the extent that the experience gained could make all the difference on the public road. If you do not know where you can receive skid pan tuition in your area, ask your local authority road safety officer.

When driving on slippery roads you must constantly be aware of how little grip your tyres have. There is far more to driving safely than knowing how to control a skid, because you must never take your car so close to the limit that a skid is possible. You must use the brakes sensitively and in good time, applying the braking techniques for wet roads described in Chapter 6 even more rigorously when driving on ice and snow. You must allow considerably greater braking distance between you and the vehicle in front, because the space needed to pull up on ice could be 10 times that required on a dry road. It is all too easy to be lulled into a false sense of security if you reach a section of road which is free from ice and snow, only to find that round the next bend the surface is just as slippery as before. You may find yourself with 50 feet in which to pull up when you need 500. Remember that speed is relatively easy to build up, but hard to take off.

Wheelspin at standstill

Even the best tyres can lose their grip and start spinning when the surface is slippery, and this can happen just as easily in summer mud as winter snow. This happens partly because the treads become filled with ice (badly worn tyres will lose their grip more quickly) and partly because water, liquid or frozen, acts as a lubricant between road and rubber.

When you find it difficult to get your car moving, the answer is to supply just enough power to the wheels to get the car rolling without causing them to spin. You must use all the finesse and sensitivity you can summon, but not be so restrained with the accelerator that the engine will stall. It is a good idea to start in second gear (or the second 'hold' on an automatic) and release the clutch gently so that the power is delivered to the driven wheels with minimum force. Should the grip be lost and the wheels start to spin, resist any inclination to press the accelerator harder to try to force the car to move. This will only make the wheels spin more vigorously and dig themselves down into the snow, making the job of getting out even more difficult. Get it wrong and you could find your car totally immobilised with its driven wheels stuck in deep ruts, when more sensitivity in the first place could have got you rolling.

You may find that you can move a foot or two before wheelspin starts. The answer is to release the power when the driven wheels start to spin, let the car roll back, dig away any loose snow and try again. If necessary, do this repeatedly by rolling back to the beginning of your wheel ruts, taking care not to allow any wheelspin which will deepen them. With patience and care, you might be able gradually to win a 'runway' with enough length for you to build up speed and escape. All the time remember that trying to 'muscle' your way out by allowing the wheels to spin on snow will only worsen your predicament. Passengers can help by spreading grit, twigs, sacks, rags, an expendable blanket or even the car's footmats under the driving wheels to improve traction, but make sure that you are well in the clear before you stop to pick up your 'tools' and passengers.

As well as using a higher gear to get you out of a tight spot, remember that the highest possible gear is always best whenever driving on ice or snow. This will prevent you from provoking a skid by feeding too much power to the driven wheels. You should try to use one higher ratio than normal, but do not let the engine labour unduly.

Reading the road

Whenever the temperature is close to freezing point, you must be prepared for slippery roads. It is vital to understand the conditions, and read the road so that you anticipate dangerous spots before they catch you out. For example, on a frosty night when major roads have been salted or gritted, do not expect minor roads to have been treated in the same way. Even on a fine day when the road surface seems normal, be aware that ice might have remained where trees and walls shade the road, or where wind sweeps across an exposed hilltop or bridge.

The notorious, and often misinterpreted, winter hazard of black ice should always be expected on a cold night, and for several hours in the morning after a cold night. Black ice occurs where water has melted during the day, spread across the road and then frozen again as the temperature drops after dusk, creating a surface like an ice rink. The danger is that you may think the surface of the road illuminated by your headlights appears to be wet, when in fact it is icy. Because it occurs in patches, it is very easy to be caught out after driving for several miles along a road which seems normal. Black ice can be very frightening and should be treated with the greatest respect.

Using your powers of observation can keep you clear of many of the problems which winter can throw at you, but just occasionally even the most sensible driver can find himself stuck fast along a quiet country road. Only you can decide whether to wait for help or to go looking for it, depending on how remote you are. This might never happen to you, but if it does you will be glad if you have been far-sighted enough to keep a shovel, wellington boots, gloves and plenty of warm clothing in your car. You can keep warm, of course, by leaving the engine running with the heater switched on, but do not make the potentially fatal mistake of leaving the engine running for too long. Exhaust gases contain poisonous carbon monoxide (with no taste or smell) which kills if you inhale enough of it. Many exhausts leak small quantities of gas which are blown away unnoticed when you are driving along, but which can seep into the passenger compartment when the car is stationary. If already tired occupants begin to doze off in the warmth, you can imagine the danger. If it really seems pointless to start walking in seek of help, rely on thick clothing as well as the car's heater to keep you warm inside, and get out periodically for a brisk walk to revive your circulation.

Summary

- Make sure that your car is *properly prepared* for winter driving.
- When roads are slippery, use all the controls – steering, brakes, accelerator, clutch – even more *smoothly and gently* than normal to avoid the danger of skidding.
- Be completely familiar with the procedures for controlling a skidding car: *steer into the skid* and *do not brake*. It is an excellent idea to take your car to a skid pan so that you learn exactly how to handle it.
- If your car is stuck in snow, use second gear and a gentle throttle to *avoid wheelspin*.
- *Read the road* to prepare yourself for slippery spots; treat the surface with the utmost respect if *black ice* seems a possibility.

16

DRIVING IN SUMMER

You might expect summer to be the easiest time of the year for driving, but do not be misled into thinking that there are no special hazards when the weather is warmer. As well as the special road conditions which can occur in summer, you should bear in mind that driving is more tiring on a bright day. Sunglasses are essential to reduce the strain on your eyes. Heat and the sun's glare also make you feel more sleepy, so stop to rest your eyes if you feel that your concentration and alertness start to suffer.

Summer driving hazards

Slippery surface

One of the most important aspects to remember about summer driving is that a film of dust, rubber and oil accumulates on road surfaces during dry weather. While this does not appreciably affect the grip of your tyres while the road remains dry, a summer shower can make this greasy coating almost as slippery as ice. The longer a spell without rain, the more treacherous the roads can be when rain does come, particularly at points where traffic is heavy: make sure that you are always aware of this phenomenon, but pay particular attention at roundabouts and through bends on roads where traffic is heavy. After a while this coating is washed away by rain so that the surface becomes less slippery, but take it easy all the time.

Overheated tarmac

A very hot day when the sun is bright can also cause the road surface to heat up to the point where tarmac begins to melt. Improved road-building techniques have made this problem less marked than it used to be, but even so a stretch of road where the surface appears to have a sheen may well not offer as much grip as usual on a very hot day, particularly if traffic is heavy. Sometimes you see signs of the road surface breaking up on bends under the pressure of heavy lorries, so remember that grip will be reduced on this bumpy, slightly molten surface.

Loose chippings
Summer is the time when many local authorities, seemingly with increasing frequency, decide to dress their roads with a layer of tar and stone chippings. While road signs and temporary speed limits are usually posted to warn you of this, many drivers under-estimate the hazards that such roads create if not treated circumspectly. Keep further back than normal from a vehicle in front to reduce the chances of flying chippings smashing your windscreen, keep your speed right down and be prepared for stones to be thrown up by any driver foolish enough to overtake. Since the surface is loose, it should go without saying that your car's tyres also will not grip so well on corners. After a while a newly-dressed surface begins to settle down, but even so you should remember that loose stones tend to accumulate at the edge of the road, creating a surface which is akin to driving on marbles.

Summer haze
The heat haze caused by hot air rising from the road's surface does not occur frequently in Britain, but take special care when considering an overtaking manoeuvre if you do see this 'shimmering' effect in the distance on a straight stretch of road. Your view of oncoming vehicles can be distorted by this illusion, giving you the wrong impression of their speed and distance.

Obscured vision
You should clean the windscreen regularly to keep it free of the dead flies and grease which accumulate so quickly in summer. It is difficult to see through a mass of squashed flies even when it is dry, but if you have to switch on your windscreen wipers during a sudden shower you will find it virtually impossible to see through the smears. A 'screen wash' liquid added to the water in the windscreen washer

reservoir will help the wipers to clear the worst of this, but even so a proper scrub is needed to do the job properly. If you are on a long journey and you find that the windscreen becomes heavily soiled, a ball of newspaper is quite effective for wiping away traffic film.

Night driving
Many people like to avoid congested roads in summer by travelling at night, particularly when going on holiday. If you ever do this, make sure that you are always alert at the wheel; pay good attention to the advice on this subject contained in Chapter 12.

Summer rain

Although it does not usually last long, a summer shower or thunderstorm can be very heavy. If your windscreen wipers have trouble coping with the deluge, it may be wise to stop the car somewhere safely off the road and wait for the rain to ease off. Rain can fall so quickly that large puddles can form at the edge of the road, perhaps where drains are blocked; in this case, slow right down to a pace which allows you to cope if suddenly faced with several inches of water under your nearside wheels. Again, it might be sensible to stop until the rain passes and you can see properly. With visibility and tyre adhesion already reduced, there is a high risk of running off the road, or even of someone less careful than yourself running into your car.

The high humidity which accompanies summer thunderstorms can make the windows of your car mist up very quickly. Use the heated rear window and windscreen demister to keep the glass clear, and if necessary open two diagonally opposite side windows to let a draught of air through the car. Rain may come through open windows, of course, but a little discomfort is preferable to the danger of trying to drive while peering through steamed-up glass.

Every now and again rain falls so heavily that roads become flooded in dips, although this occurs more often in winter when the ground is water-logged. Floods and fords can be negotiated quite easily as long as you observe some basic rules. Your main concern will be whether you can drive through without affecting the engine; some cars can cope with more than a foot of water, but you would be stupid to try if the water is likely to reach above the base of the doors. If driving through the flood means that water will reach the bottom of the engine cooling fan, do not attempt it as the fan blades will throw water round the engine bay and drown the ignition. If you are in any doubt, it would be far more sensible to turn round and find another route.

Try to assess the depth of water from banks, hedges and even buildings. While you are wondering whether to venture through, it is quite likely that another driver, perhaps one in a vehicle with more ground clearance, will have a go; this will give you a very good idea of the depth of water. If you are convinced the water is shallow enough to be negotiated, start in first gear and keep the revs high – by slipping the clutch if you have to – to prevent water entering the exhaust pipe and stifling the engine. Drive into the water slowly so that you do not create a bow wave which could force its way into the engine bay.

Despite taking all these precautions, you may still find yourself stranded because water drowns the ignition system and the engine dies. In this case you can attempt to drive the car out on the starter motor (unless your car has an automatic gearbox), although this involves ill-treatment of the engine. Simply engage first gear and keep the starter turning to propel the car slowly and jerkily forwards, stopping every 15 seconds or so to let the starter motor cool down. This will eventually get you to dry land, but you will be kicking yourself that you did not decide to turn round and find another route. There is really no point in taking any chances when for the sake of a few lost minutes you could take an alternative road, navigating by sense of direction if necessary.

Once you are clear of the flood water, waste no time in trying the brakes repeatedly and firmly while driving slowly away. Water on the surfaces of the brakes makes them virtually useless until you have dried them with a few hard jabs of the pedal. Disc brakes return to normal power quite quickly, but water lingers far longer in drums, which are used at the rear on many cars. Do drive slowly while you do this, and avoid surprising any other drivers behind you.

Summary

- Bear in mind the hazards of summer driving: allow for *greasy roads* when rain falls after a long dry spell; take special care when *loose chippings* have been laid as a surface dressing; keep your *windscreen* clear of dead flies and grime.
- Drive very carefully in the heavy rain of a *summer storm*; visibility can be poor, and deep surface water can lie on the road.
- When you come across a *flooded road*, satisfy yourself that your car will go through the water safely; drive very slowly in first gear, keeping the revs high.

17

DRIVING FOR ECONOMY

Ever since the oil crisis of the early 1970s, everybody has become more interested in fuel economy. Motorists have been forced to take more notice of it because fuel has become relatively expensive, and car manufacturers have answered this by concentrating more of their research and development on engine efficiency and aerodynamics. By and large, cars are more economical than they have ever been, but there is one person who can have a more dramatic effect than a whole team of engineers – you.

Although it is to be encouraged, however, driving for economy must never be allowed to come before considerations of safety. It is quite conceivable that a driver can find himself in a potentially dangerous situation, perhaps through being unwilling to accelerate briskly when it is necessary, simply because he has allowed petrol saving to become more important than planned, systematic and constructive advanced driving. Nevertheless, the basic principles of advanced driving tend to go hand in hand with economical motoring: anticipating hazards well in advance, braking in good time and using the accelerator smoothly and progressively all contribute to economical driving.

Do's and don'ts

There are a number of points to remember when trying to make the most of each precious gallon of fuel:

- *Don't* inflate the tyres to a higher pressure than that recommended by the manufacturer. Extra tyre wear will far outweigh the tiny amount of petrol saved, and the smaller contact patches of your car's tyres will affect steering, roadholding and braking because grip is reduced.

- *Don't* use cheaper two-star fuel if your car should run on four-star, because the engine can be damaged by this false economy. A cheaper grade will probably cause 'pinking' – the destructive pre-ignition during acceleration which is apparent from a faint tinkling noise.

- *Don't* stay in a high gear when road speed demands a lower gear. This not only means that you disregard the basic advanced driving principle of being in the right gear at the right time, but it is also mechanically unsympathetic because it makes the engine labour.

- *Don't* coast in neutral, either when driving downhill or when coming to a stop. Having the gearbox in neutral means that your response is delayed if it is necessary suddenly to accelerate out of trouble.

- *Don't* drive too slowly, as this makes you an unnecessary hazard to other road users.

- *Do* keep your speed down to what seems a minimum reasonable level, so that you save fuel without being a nuisance to other road users.

- *Do* avoid revving the engine too fast or accelerating too hard, except when road and traffic conditions demand it.

- *Do* make sure, if your car has a manual choke, that it is closed as soon as possible after a cold start, but not so soon that the engine refuses to run properly. Remember that closing it too early causes the engine to falter and possibly to stall, which can be very dangerous at a junction.

The car you buy

The type of car you run, as much as the way in which you drive it, will influence fuel consumption so there is no point in buying a car with a larger or more powerful engine than you need. Look at the choice of engine sizes available for the model you choose and try to work out which suits you best, remembering that a smaller unit will not always be more economical. Since a smaller engine has to work harder in certain conditions, it can end up using as much fuel in practice as a larger but under-worked engine. Most cars these days have five-speed gearboxes, but if a five-speed is only optional for your chosen model it is worth asking yourself whether the extra cost would be worthwhile for the sake of 'long-legged' – and therefore more economical – cruising.

Compare the fuel consumption figures of the cars on your short list before making your decision. EC rules oblige every manufacturer to quote fuel consumption figures for a standard urban cycle, steady 56mph and steady 75mph, so these can act as a guide. These figures appear in some of the motoring magazines, in manufacturers' brochures and in the Institute of Advanced Motorists' own *Milestones* magazine. But do not be misled by a particularly good steady 56mph figure, for this would be almost impossible to attain in normal traffic conditions; the steady 75mph figure is likely to be closer to what you can reasonably expect in day-to-day driving.

By the way, you may have wondered why 75mph is always quoted when our national speed limit (on dual-carriageways and motorways) is 70mph. The answer is that 75mph equates to 120kph (a legal speed in most European countries), a figure which the EC has deemed suitable as a fuel consumption yardstick. Road tests in motoring magazines usually state the fuel consumption achieved through the duration of the test, but bear in mind that this will reflect plenty of hard driving off public roads to obtain performance figures; magazine figures will invariably be less than you will achieve, but they can be useful in comparing one car with another.

Unleaded fuel

At the time of writing, a tax concession makes unleaded fuel cheaper than normal leaded grades, and this situation seems likely to continue at least until regulations require all new cars to run on unleaded fuel. Apart from playing your own part in reducing atmospheric pollution, therefore, you can also save money by running your car on unleaded fuel. Before doing so, however, check with your dealer whether your car can already run on unleaded fuel, or whether it needs adjustment first. The cost of any adjustment will be recouped fairly quickly, but do not be surprised if this is not possible because a few cars cannot be altered to take unleaded fuel. There may be a slight power loss, but you are unlikely to notice it.

Diesel or petrol?
The increasing popularity of diesel-engined cars shows that many motorists choose them because of their longer engine life and greater economy. The disadvantages are that diesels are noisier (although modern diesels have become much quieter), offer less performance and cost more to buy. Diesel fuel is cheaper and goes as much as 40 per cent further, but generally speaking the higher purchase price of diesel cars makes them suitable only for drivers covering a high mileage. You will have to weigh up the costs for yourself before making your decision, but do not dismiss a diesel on the grounds that it is noisy and smelly until you have tried one for yourself – you may be surprised by the refinement of the best modern diesel cars.

Service
Following the manufacturer's recommended service intervals religiously will keep your car's engine running in the best state of tune. Maladjusted ignition and carburettors, as well as worn spark plugs, can affect fuel economy adversely. A normal service should also include a check of the brakes and wheel alignment; any problems here can add to the resistance which your car's engine must overcome to propel it.

Economy devices
There was a time when accessory economy devices were popular, but motor manufacturers have made such strides in improving engine efficiency that these are really not worth considering nowadays. The only accessory which you might find useful is an 'engine efficiency meter' or vacuum gauge, an instrument which measures the depression in the inlet manifold and translates this into a simple display of information on a dial. By keeping the accelerator opening balanced against road and engine speed, you can keep the needle in the sector of the dial

which shows that you are making best use of the fuel, although you should never forget considerations of safety.

The best economy device is free – your right foot. You can save a great deal of fuel by avoiding excessive acceleration, easing off well before any hazard and feathering the accelerator back at cruising speeds. A car will cruise comfortably along a level road with a surprisingly small throttle opening. Putting your foot further down will bring only a slight increase in speed and much heavier fuel consumption.

Summary

- While the principles of *advanced driving* generally help fuel economy, think about how you can use the advice in this chapter to improve economy still further; but avoid putting economy before safety and driving slowly enough to be a nuisance to other road-users.
- Think about fuel economy when you *choose your car*. What size engine? Petrol or diesel? Can I use unleaded fuel?

18

TRAFFIC

Just occasionally all of us find the pleasure of motoring heightened by a drive through beautiful countryside on quiet roads, but most of the time we have to contend with other traffic, and an increasing quantity of it. Sometimes, however, you may be able to make what promises to be a congested journey more enjoyable by re-timing it (perhaps by leaving home before the rush hour or after it subsides) or by planning to by-pass towns wherever possible (by travelling on country roads as well as purpose-built by-passes). By carefully studying a map before a long journey, you may be able to avoid much of the traffic.

Using maps

If your route leaves you no alternative to driving through congested areas, there are ways in which you can make life a little easier for yourself. For example, you can reduce the amount of concentration needed for navigation by getting a passenger to guide you along unfamiliar roads or through a strange town. The excellent large-format paperback road atlases now available are updated annually so that you can be sure all the new roads are shown if you have a recent copy, and many of these atlases also contain street maps for larger towns and cities.

If you are driving alone, it is a very good idea to plan your route in advance and write on a piece of paper all the important towns and road numbers to look for. By glancing at this at traffic lights you have an instant route-finder at your fingertips, thereby saving yourself the bother of frequent stops – and of finding somewhere safe to stop – in order to thumb through an atlas. A route card, perhaps written on the back of a postcard, might look like this:

At J14 (Hungerford) of M4 turn l. onto A338
1 mile later turn r. onto B4000
7 miles later bear l. onto A4, towards Newbury
At first roundabout in Newbury, turn l. on Wantage
road
Almost immediately, turn 1. into Donnington Square.

With the aid of a good-scale map, such as the large-format paperback atlases mentioned above, you will be able to estimate distances fairly accurately. By keeping an eye on your car's mileage recorder, you can give yourself plenty of warning about when your next junction can be expected.

Using lanes

Since driving in traffic is a fact of motoring life, you must learn to live with it. You must gain the keen awareness which allows an advanced driver to handle his car in traffic confidently and safely, yet you must also guard against the dangerous over-confidence which some drivers seem to acquire as they become familiar with heavy traffic conditions.

Heavy main road and motorway traffic, with two or three lanes of traffic travelling along at anything up to 70mph, is usually the most daunting to the novice driver. At busy times of day you are likely to see only a few drivers maintaining a proper distance behind the vehicle in front, but you must try to stick to this safe rule at all times, even if it means that other drivers sometimes slot into the sensible space you have left. When this happens you must drop back to re-establish the safe distance: this proper sense of caution will make little difference to your journey time, but it could make all the difference in keeping you – and others – out of trouble if an accident happens ahead. Serious pile-ups on motorways or dual carriageways would not happen if every driver observed this basic rule of good driving.

When traffic in two or more lanes is flowing at similar speeds, you often see the type of hooligan driver who switches lanes to put himself in whichever seems the best one at any given moment. This behaviour occurs most frequently on urban dual carriageways, and it seems increasingly to be regarded as almost acceptable – although it certainly raises the level of danger – on the busiest of them. The basic rule, of course, is that you stay in the left-hand lane unless you have a specific reason for occupying another one. On a very busy three-lane urban road with plenty of heavy lorries and buses occupying the left-hand lane, as well as the occasional driver intending to turn left, you will probably spend most, if not all, of your time in the centre lane, leaving the right-hand lane for drivers who are overtaking or planning to turn right. It is advisable to treat two-lane roads as though the right-hand and centre lanes were combined.

If everybody followed this pattern these roads would be more straightforward to cope with, but you will inevitably meet with a cut-and-thrust attitude. A typical example might come from the driver who has tried to make faster progress in the right-hand lane only to find that he wants a way back into the centre lane when he comes up behind someone turning right.

You should always stay in the inside lane, therefore, unless you have a good reason to move temporarily to another one. But do follow another basic principle of advanced driving by keeping an eye on what is going on well ahead, so that you have plenty of time to judge any change of lane. Apart from overtaking slower vehicles, a lane-change might become necessary because a three-lane road narrows down to two lanes, or because a left-turn filter allows vehicles to peel off early approaching a junction (especially those controlled by lights). If you find yourself in a left-hand filter lane when you wish to go straight on, it is best to make the turn and then return to your route by side roads or by finding somewhere safe to turn round. To make a sudden, unplanned lane-change is dangerous, and to sit at a green filter light blocking the path of other drivers is discourteous.

Very often you can find yourself driving in the left or centre lane as part of a flow of traffic which is moving more quickly than the stream to your right: in effect, you find yourself obliged to overtake on the inside, albeit usually at a speed which means that you pass the vehicle to your right quite gradually. This is permissible because modern traffic density has forced it to be so, but you must never step over the borderline (admittedly a slightly indistinct one) and start indulging in deliberate 'inside overtaking'. Not only is this illegal, but it is also highly dangerous because the driver you pass may be taken by surprise. It is also illegal, and equally stupid, to use the hard shoulder to pass other vehicles on a motorway.

It is permissible to overtake on the left along a one-way street, but remember that doing so can take other road users and pedestrians by surprise. You should keep to the left along a one-way street unless this lane is heading towards a left turn or you plan to make a right turn yourself.

Always take special care when coming up behind traffic waiting to turn right. The road lay-out may give you room to slip through if you have failed to anticipate the situation, but do so with great caution. A pedestrian might be about to step out between stationary vehicles without expecting to meet a moving car, or a driver in the queue waiting to turn right might suddenly decide to drive straight on and move into your path.

Pedestrian crossings on urban roads with two or more lanes are very dangerous places, for drivers as well as pedestrians. Stop in good time when you see someone wishing to cross, and always be prepared for the possibility of one of the drivers ahead of you making a sudden decision to stop for a pedestrian to cross. It is a serious offence to overtake anyone on the approach to a pedestrian crossing, that is in the area marked by zig-zag white lines at the side of the road.

Stopping in traffic

Keep checking your mirror when you are at a standstill, even at traffic lights. If a driver in your mirror appears to be coming up too quickly, a few dabs on the brake pedal will flash your brake lights to alert him to your presence.

When you stop at traffic lights, you should apply the handbrake and put the gear lever into neutral. As soon as you see the amber to green sequence, engage first gear and prepare to release the handbrake ready to move off when the green light appears. Many motorists waste their own time and that of other road-users – as well as reducing the number of vehicles able to pass through a busy junction in each sequence – by delaying these actions until the green light actually appears. Rather than gazing around, watch the lights while you are waiting so that you are ready to move off smartly; it is a good idea, if you can see them, to watch the lights controlling other streams of traffic so that you have a few seconds' warning of when your lights will change.

Oil accumulates on the road at any places where vehicles regularly stop, so allow for the possibility of greatly reduced tyre grip, whether you are braking to a stop or accelerating away again. The coating of oil and rubber on city streets tends to become polished by constant traffic, so remember that urban road surfaces can be very slippery in wet weather.

Pay special attention to pedestrians when negotiating junctions in towns, especially where they cross at traffic lights. People can quite easily step into the road without glancing to see whether it is clear, and if a large number of pedestrians is streaming across in front of you it is quite possible that a few tail-enders following the flock will cross as your lights are changing to green. Beware of the cyclist who emerges from a side street without looking, and never forget that any cyclist is entitled to his wobble, as a High Court ruling has confirmed. It is the motorist's responsibility to avoid a cyclist.

It should go without saying that nipping through traffic lights as the signal changes from amber to red is terribly dangerous; just as risky is anticipating the green by moving away when you see the amber. You can imagine the dangerous consequences when two 'amber gamblers' meet in the middle of a junction. Remember that the green light should be taken as permission to continue with caution, not an instruction to proceed.

If you have stopped on a hill, always allow a little extra room in case the vehicle in front should roll back. The driver may not have applied the handbrake firmly enough, or may make such a clumsy start that his vehicle rolls back a couple of feet before it moves forward. A warning toot on the horn will probably prevent a gentle impact if you see this start to happen, but if you leave it too late, or if you have not left those extra few feet as a margin, the vehicle may hit your car. Easing off your own brake a fraction can ease the impact, but take care not to roll back yourself. The fact that learners – and some more experienced drivers – have been known to select reverse instead of first emphasises the value of leaving that extra gap when you have to wait in traffic on a hill.

Another point to remember when stopping on a hill is that you should never hold the car on the clutch: always use the handbrake. Apart from the danger of stalling the engine and letting the car roll back, or even of a sudden surge forward if your foot slips, using the clutch in this way will wear it out rapidly.

Parking

There are two important rules concerning parking. First, observe the law, even if you feel that it seems unreasonable (remember that parking restrictions are intended to ease the flow of traffic, and sometimes to discourage people from bringing their cars into town centres). Second, be thoughtful about the safety and convenience of other drivers and pedestrians. This consideration will mean that you avoid parking close to junctions, a common problem which inconveniences drivers making a turn and gives a dangerously restricted view for any driver trying to pull out into the traffic. You should also avoid parking in front of someone's drive, or at a popular crossing point where pedestrians would have to funnel round your car.

The technique of parking is extremely simple, yet it seems to evade many people throughout their motoring lives. The golden rule is not to enter a space nose first, unless it is a really large space. You should drive alongside a chosen space, assessing whether it is long enough to take your car, and stop when your own car's rear wheels are alongside the back of the parked car ahead of your space, keeping about two feet out. Reverse slowly on full left-lock (for a space on the left-hand side of the road), switching to full right-lock as the front of your car clears the one ahead. It helps, of course, to have a very clear idea of the exact

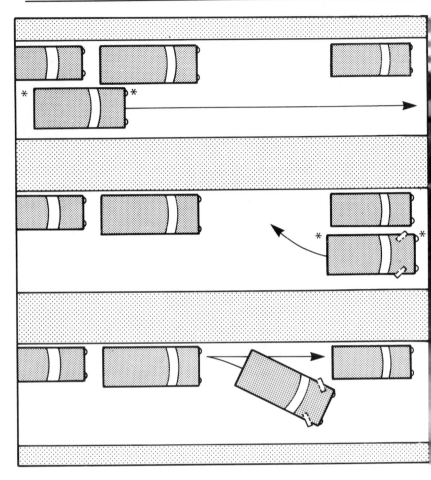

Parking in a restricted space. This is one manoeuvre which many drivers never master, yet it is simple, and is a good way of demonstrating a driver's spatial concepts. Provided that you have judged the available space accurately, this procedure should be completed in two movements – first backwards then forwards – though a bit of juggling might be called for in a really tight situation.

position of the invisible front extremities of your car. Perform this manoeuvre correctly with one smooth movement and you will end up with all four wheels neatly adjacent to the kerb. It then remains only to edge forward a few feet with the steering wheel centred to place your car in the middle of the space. With practice, you will be able to park your car in surprisingly small gaps.

Before we leave the subject of traffic, it is worth observing that people used to driving in the very dense, sometimes swift-moving traffic of large cities are generally more confident. London drivers, in particular, seem to have a decisive style which seems almost foolhardy to drivers from quieter parts of the country, but by and large it works well because they know what they are doing and where they are going. The press-on approach helps to move large volumes of traffic through some very congested road systems.

Applying the same decisive style on a provincial town's roads can seem aggressive, even downright dangerous, partly because it is out of place. In the same way, someone driving warily in London for the first time must try not to be intimidated by the cut-and-thrust of somewhere like Hyde Park Corner in the rush hour. Each type of driving is right for the conditions, so it can be dangerous if you do not – or even feel that you cannot – conform to the traffic pattern around you. The advice can really only be this: 'When in Rome, do as the Romans do'.

Summary

- If you plan to make a journey along unfamiliar roads, prepare a *route card* to ease the task of navigation.
- Always maintain the required *braking distance* when traffic is very heavy, even if this means dropping back when another vehicle nips into the space you have left.
- Use all your powers of observation on a busy two- or three-lane road so that you are never *caught in the wrong lane*: look out for traffic turning left or right; prepare to overtake a slow-moving vehicle well in advance; avoid becoming obliged to take an unwanted left-hand filter lane.
- Treat *traffic lights* responsibly; when traffic is heavy, you should help the flow through a junction by being

ready to move off smartly when the green light appears.

- Teach yourself to park properly: a good *parking technique* helps you and causes less delay to other drivers.

19

MOTORWAYS

Few drivers seem to have a good word for motorways these days, moaning about congestion on some of our more notorious stretches, the tedium of driving on them, and the frequency of roadworks. Yet motorways have allowed motorists to make a long journey in a time which would have seemed inconceivable 30 years ago.

Much of the rather morbid mystique associated with motorways can be blamed on the media, because a motorway accident is sufficiently catastrophic for television and newspapers to focus their attention on it. As a result, it is often forgotten that motorways have a lower accident record than other main roads. Since the chances of an accident on a motorway are much lower than one on a comparable non-motorway trunk road, it provides a safer route, as well as a quicker one, to your destination.

Speeds on motorways are such, however, that great discipline is required to use them safely. You must stick to the rules, and in doing so you might help to avoid some of the disasters which a few motorway hooligans seem determined to cause. You will encounter plenty of bad driving on motorways: the advice which follows will help you to make sure that your own driving is responsible and safe, even if others fail to meet the standard. The Institute's views on motorway driving, of course, follow the rules and guidelines described in the *Highway Code*, but to these basics can be added the wisdom gained from experience. Our advice is influenced by the comments we have obtained from the most professional of all professional drivers – the police patrol officers.

Motorways have two great advantages: they are one-way and there are no junctions, so you should not have someone coming towards you or nipping across in front of you. It is just possible, though, that one day in your driving life you may meet a driver who is dim enough to break these most fundamental rules. There have been incidents, some resulting in fatalities, of drivers making a U-turn through the central reservation after missing their exit. There have also been cases of drivers somehow managing to proceed along an exit slip road in the wrong direction and meet oncoming traffic when they reach the carriageway. If you should be unlucky enough to meet a driver such as this, we can only recommend that you take avoiding action, flash your headlights and blast your horn, and stop at the next emergency telephone (these are a mile apart) to inform the police.

Terminology

Before dealing with the techniques of advanced driving on motorways, some brief words are necessary about terminology. Some drivers describe the three lanes of a motorway as the 'slow', 'middle' and 'fast' lanes: this is misleading, since speed alone does not determine the use of lanes, and to describe a lane as 'fast' smacks of irresponsibility. More usual practice is to use the terms 'inside', 'centre' and 'outside', but as more and more motorway sections with four lanes are being constructed this nomenclature is becoming outdated and could be confusing. The best way is the notation used by the police, and this is what we shall follow in this chapter. Each lane is simply given a number: therefore, lane 1 is the 'inside', lane 2 the 'centre' and lane 3 the 'outside', with lane 4 used where applicable.

Joining a motorway

The motorway slip road should be used to accelerate to a speed which matches that of the traffic in lane 1. Signal a right turn so that anyone in lane 1 will notice you, and will maybe move over to lane 2 to give you plenty of room. Your run along the stretch of the slip road adjoining the main carriageway should be timed so that you can slip neatly into place as soon as possible without losing speed, but keep a wary eye on the timid driver who may be slowing down at the end of the slip road to wait for a large gap in the traffic. In extreme cases, this kind of driver –

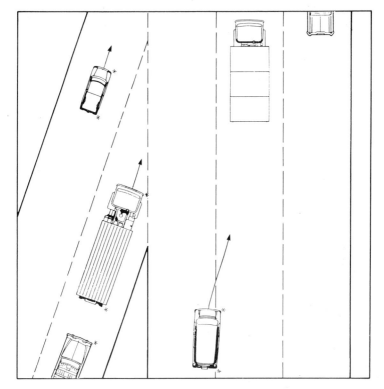

When joining a motorway by a slip road your speed should match that of the traffic in lane 1. You should remain in lane 1 for at least half a mile before moving into lane 2.

who is as much of a menace to himself as to other road-users – may even stop at the end of the slip road, as if to give way.

You should remain in lane 1 for at least half a mile to adjust yourself to the speed and assess the traffic pattern behind you. If you are driving a car (rather than a lorry, or a car towing a caravan), your cruising speed will probably mean that you will spend a good proportion of your motorway journey in lane 2, so move over, after the usual mirror check and right turn signal, when it becomes necessary. Return to lane 1 whenever it is reasonably clear after overtaking manoeuvres have been completed. Lane 3 is *not* the fast lane which many people take it to be, so use it only for overtaking.

Motorway discipline

Your speed along a motorway should be one at which you, your passengers and the car feel comfortable, and one which is appropriate to weather conditions and traffic density – but it must not be over 70mph. You should not drive so unreasonably slowly along a motorway that you inconvenience other drivers coming up behind, but neither should you treat 70mph as an obligatory speed: 70mph is a limit, not a target. Travelling a few miles per hour under the limit will make little difference to your journey time.

If a motorist comes up behind travelling at more than 70mph, it is not your job to uphold the law. Baulking an overtaking driver, whether or not he is travelling at a legal speed, can be dangerous as well as discourteous, and the police would not thank you for it.

Lane discipline

Once you have settled into a steady cruising speed, glance in the mirror frequently so that you are constantly aware of all the vehicles around you. Maintain strict lane discipline, so that you are always in the appropriate lane for your speed and the traffic conditions. Poor lane discipline is one of the most common examples of bad driving on motorways, and it can occasionally play its part in an accident when it forces drivers unnecessarily into lane 3. Far too often on motorways you see more traffic travelling in lane 3 than in lanes 1 and 2. If there is a reasonable break in the traffic in lane 1, that is where you should be.

If you come up behind a 'lane hog' who fails to move over when there is plenty of space available, do not resort to the aggressive tactics which many drivers employ. Remember that the principles of good driving require you to maintain a proper braking distance, so never be tempted to force a slower vehicle aside by looming large in the driver's mirrors. Be patient and wait for the opportunity to overtake safely. Never overtake on the inside: as well as being a serious offence, this can be dangerous since no driver expects it to happen.

Keep your distance

Keeping a safe distance between you and the vehicle in front is even more important than good lane discipline. The importance of leaving room for seeing, reacting and braking has already been explained elsewhere in this book, but maintaining a safe distance is particularly relevant on a motorway. It is all too easy to close up on the vehicle ahead so that the distance between you is nothing like adequate in an emergency, so keep reminding yourself of this point. Drivers stopped by the police for driving extremely close, or 'tailgating', often use the excuse that they can see several vehicles ahead, but they are deluding themselves. This foolish attitude ignores all kinds of possibilities: the driver ahead might brake suddenly if he sees a piece of debris in the road, a vehicle from the opposing carriageway might crash through the central reservation, or the vehicle ahead might even suffer a tyre blow-out. Another reason why people fail to keep a safe gap is that overtaking vehicles often slot into the space you have allowed; all you can do is drop back accordingly.

Slip road courtesy

As you approach and pass an entrance slip road, it is necessary to keep an eye on any traffic which may be about to join the motorway. If it is quite safe for you to move from lane 1 to lane 2 without obstructing a driver coming up behind, it is courteous to do so in order to make life easier for drivers joining the motorway; this forethought will be especially appreciated by lorry drivers, who are less able to adjust their speed to blend into the traffic flow. If a junction is very busy, this tactic is particularly appropriate.

Abnormal motorway conditions

A multiple pile-up on a fogbound motorway occurs almost every winter because so many people drive too fast for the conditions. But there is rather more to it than this. Many drivers make a dangerous assumption when they judge how far they should be behind the vehicle in front: they think that the distance they leave gives them room to react when brake lights appear on any of the vehicles visible in front. What this attitude does not allow for is the very real possibility that the cars in front will come to a stop instantaneously and without warning if they pile into a mass of wrecked vehicles. In fog, you must allow for the stopping distance you need *under those conditions.*

Motorway fog

Driving in fog on a motorway in other respects is governed by just the same rules which apply to fog driving on any other roads: keep down to a speed which gives safe braking distance within your range of vision; try to keep to lane 1 or 2 (and, in very thick fog, make sure you always know which lane you are in); use dipped beam headlights day or night and fog lamps if you have them (remember that it is just as important to be seen as to see); open the windows, turn on the demister and heated rear window, and use the wipers to keep the windscreen free of moisture.

Above all, be philosophical about the delay to your journey. Rather than risk being a victim in a nose-to-tail crash, it would be better to leave the motorway at the next exit and wait for the fog to clear, even if this means spending a night away from home.

You should not restrict the use of dipped headlights in daylight to foggy conditions. The law requires you to switch on dipped headlights whenever visibility is seriously diminished (defined in the *Highway Code* as less than 100 metres), so this means in heavy rain as well as fog. You must use your discretion in this matter, remembering that the object is for other road-users to see you, not necessarily to help you to see. Next time you are driving in poor conditions, notice how difficult it is to spot a vehicle without headlights when most have them switched on; headlights attract attention in the rear-view mirror, so drivers ahead will have good warning when you come up behind. Use your car's rear fog lights only when visibility is reduced to around 100 metres, and do not forget to switch them off again when conditions improve.

Motorway warning signals
Automatic motorway signals give you a recommended maximum speed during fog, on the approach to an incident or even during heavy rain, as well as giving warning of lane closures ahead or even the need to stop or leave the motorway in the event of a serious accident. Many

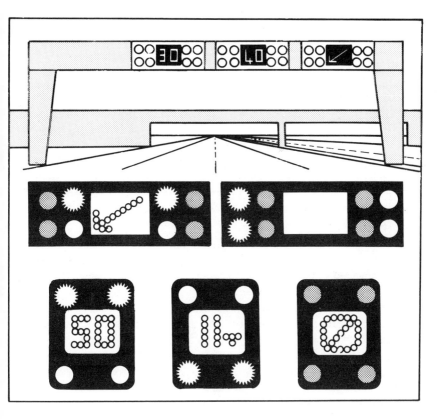

Some motorway signs. The top part of this diagram illustrates the gantry which displays the signs, which in this case are showing speed restrictions and an imminent lane closure on a three-lane carriageway. The central part of the drawing shows how the various restrictions are accompanied by flashing lights. The lower part shows other signs that you may come across on the motorway, displaying, left to right: temporary speed limit, lane 3 closed ahead, and the 'clearway' sign, which is not accompanied by flashing lights, to show that the temporary restrictions have finished.

motorists do not understand these signals, so it is worth studying the range of warnings shown in the accompanying diagram. Some drivers, furthermore, do not respect these signals, believing that they have been left on by mistake if no obvious need for them can be seen. It is worth confirming, therefore, that the police are extremely diligent in employing these signals when they are necessary and in switching them off as soon as a hazard is cleared. Always obey them, because they serve as warning that you are approaching a hazard, perhaps a mile or two down the carriageway.

These warning signals are so often abused that you may see in your rear-view mirror a car closing quite quickly. Since it is very difficult to judge the speed of a vehicle approaching from behind, it pays to exercise extreme caution and delay any planned lane-change of your own until it is well out of the way. If the signals show that you will need to make a lane-change, perhaps because an accident has blocked one or two lanes, make your manoeuvre in good time and keep below the speed indicated. Keep a careful eye open for the fast-approaching driver in an empty lane who drives dangerously into the slowing traffic stream at the last minute.

Crosswinds

Since speeds are normally higher on motorways, you need to be alert to the effect of crosswinds on your car's stability. You may feel this where a motorway crosses open country or a bridge; or you may notice buffeting as a fast-moving coach or lorry passes you. As soon as you feel a crosswind tugging at your car, reduce your speed to a point where you can steer a straight course despite the gust. A light touch on the wheel is important, as too firm a hold will remove the sensitivity of control you need to make small steering corrections.

It is also possible to adapt quite unconsciously to a sustained crosswind by applying a degree or two of lock into the wind to keep your car travelling in a straight line. Be aware of any circumstances where a steady wind may temporarily be shielded from your car, perhaps when passing a heavy lorry or driving through a cutting. You need to be prepared for this by gently correcting the steering as the pressure drops and re-applying your corrective lock when it picks up again. Without this anticipation on your part, your car could swing a few yards across the road – and perhaps alarm other road-users – before you manage to correct it.

Leaving the motorway

Taking an exit from a motorway involves a very simple procedure. Generally junction signs are posted 1-mile and ½-mile in advance, followed by three-, two- and one-bar signs which provide a countdown starting at 300 yards. It is obvious that you must synchronise your speed with the traffic in lane 1, making sure that you have completed your manoeuvre into this lane well before the three-bar sign appears; in very heavy traffic, you should slot into lane 1 (after checking your mirror and signalling a left turn) even earlier than this, soon after the 1-mile sign if necessary. If you are already travelling in lane 1, signal a left turn in good time, and certainly before you pass the three-bar sign.

Entering the slip road is a potentially hazardous moment. After driving for maybe a couple of hours at close to the legal limit, your judgement of speed will have become distorted. Since 50mph will seem more like 30mph, it is very easy to approach the roundabout too quickly and end up having to brake heavily. Some slip roads curve so sharply that the dangers of misjudging your braking become even greater. Rely on your car's speedometer as well as your judgement when making this big speed adjustment.

While on the subject of judging speed, it is worth pointing out that it is possible to become 'speed happy' while you are still on the motorway. We have already described the tendency for your judgement of braking distance to lapse, but you should also remember that a violent swerve in an emergency could cause you to lose control of your car, simply because you attempt a manoeuvre which you would never normally contemplate at such high speed.

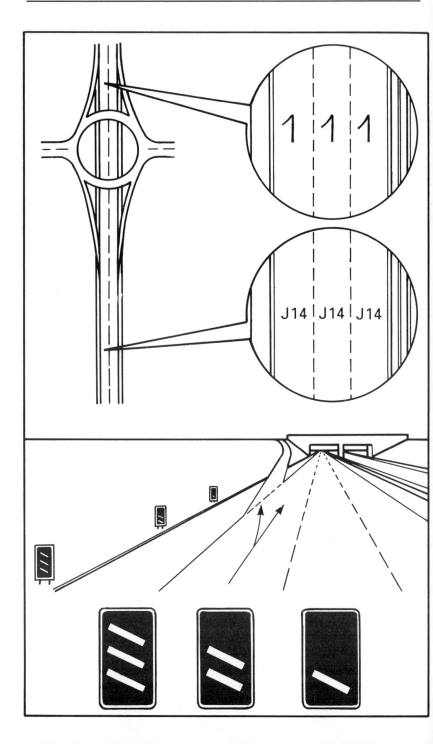

Keeping your car in trim

Once motorways have become a normal part of your driving, guarding against all these hazards should become built in to your approach as you follow the techniques of advanced driving. All that remains is to make sure that your car is able to cope as well as you are. Although you probably keep your car in good trim, a few points are worth noting.

To give their best at prolonged high speed, tyres sometimes need to be pumped up slightly harder than normal. Our speed limits and the frequency with which drivers hop on and off motorways mean that this precaution is more appropriate to driving on the continent, but the higher speeds of motorways do mean that checking the pressure and condition of your tyres becomes even more important. Analyses of motorway accidents have shown that one in six is caused by a tyre failure, so pay good attention to your tyres in order to minimise this chance. A damaged tyre is most likely to puncture or explode at high speed, when the operating temperature rises. If you are unfortunate enough to suffer a puncture on a motorway, brake gently and steer delicately to reduce the chance of the tyre peeling off the rim and rendering your car totally uncontrollable.

Many luxury cars are equipped with cruise control devices, which enable a constant speed to be maintained until overriden by the first touch on the brake or accelerator pedals. In safety terms, there is no reason why a cruise control should not be used, as long as it does not lead you to relax your vigilance; remember that it is all too easy for motorway driving to become almost mesmeric. You should never move your feet away from the pedals

Carriageway markings on a motorway include a warning that a junction is near (J14 in this case) and, once the junction is passed, a half-chevron indicating that traffic is merging from the left. The distance markers (below) are not restricted to motorways, and indicate the distance, in hundreds of yards, to the next point at which a driver may leave a motorway or other route, or a roundabout.

when using cruise control, since this delays your reaction to an emergency and may even cause you to hit the wrong pedal in haste.

Motorway breakdowns are often caused by factors which a diligent driver can avoid. Do not push a car beyond its limitations in age and design, and make sure that you have plenty of petrol and oil. Listen for any unfamiliar sounds or vibrations which may signal a mechanical problem. Remember that high speed puts more stress on your car, so the chances of mechanical failure increase on a motorway.

If you are ever forced to stop on a motorway, pull over to the far left of the hard shoulder; use of the hard shoulder, of course, is permissible only in an emergency. Turn on the hazard warning lights and sidelights to warn other road-users, and either stay in the car to wait for a police patrol vehicle or start walking to the nearest emergency telephone. Red arrows on the marker posts (at 100 metre intervals) indicate the direction of the nearest one, which will never be more than half a mile away. Keep well to the left as you walk, and tell your passengers to wait on the hard shoulder, or even the verge; leave any pets in the car. When you are able to resume your journey, do not pull straight on to the main carriageway after moving off; treat the hard shoulder as an acceleration lane, making your move to lane 1 only when your speed matches that of the vehicles around you.

Summary

- When *joining a motorway*, accelerate up the slip road to a speed which matches that of the traffic in lane 1 and move into this lane when it is safe to do so.
- Treat the 70mph speed limit *as a limit*, not as a target which you must reach.
- Remember the two essential disciplines of motorway driving: maintain a *safe braking distance* at all times and watch your *lane discipline*.
- Treat *fog* with great respect: drive at a *low speed* which allows you to stop within the range of your vision, and maintain a *braking distance* sufficient to

give you room if the vehicle ahead stops instantaneously in a crash.

- Motorway *warning signals* are always illuminated for a reason: obey them at all times.
- When planning to *leave a motorway*, ensure that you have slotted into lane 1 well before the three-bar sign.

20

FOG

While fog occurs most frequently during the winter, it should be treated as a hazard which can be encountered at any time of year. The weather can be misty even in summer, and sea fog is always a possibility on a coastal road. The simple answer to the problem of driving in fog is *don't*, but there will always be occasions, for example if a journey is essential or you are caught on the road, when you have to drive on. However, if fog is really dense, bear in mind that an unscheduled stop in a hotel is infinitely preferable to a spell in hospital.

Speed

The basic rule for driving in fog is that you must reduce your speed so that you can stop within the range of your vision, even if this means a speed of only 5mph. Of course, such a low speed would probably make it pointless to persevere with your journey. You are asking for trouble if you attempt to drive faster than 'braking distance rate'; before long you will collide with something or someone.

Some drivers are tempted to pick up a white line and follow it blindly. You may be lucky and get away with this technique for years, but eventually you will crash into the back of a stationary, unlit vehicle. White lines and cats eyes should be used only as a guide to where the road goes, so rely instead on your own eyesight. Never straddle a centre white line – you might meet someone coming the other way doing exactly the same thing.

Always be prepared to find somewhere safe to stop and wait for the fog to lift if it is very dense. Do not park where another vehicle might run into the back of you, and leave your sidelights and hazard warning lights switched on.

Lights

Always keep your car's headlights on dipped beam in fog whether it is day or night; *never* drive on sidelights alone. It is absolutely vital in fog that other drivers should have maximum warning of your approach, so the dipped headlight rule exists in order that your vehicle is seen, not necessarily for you to see. It is better to avoid using main beam, because fog reflects so much light that dipped beam generally gives you a better view. Fog lamps, if you have them, are designed to give better light penetration in fog.

Junctions are particularly hazardous in fog, so a safe rule is to flash your lights and sound your horn when you have to cross the path of other vehicles which may be hidden in the fog; it is best to wind down your window so that you can listen too. Exercise special care when turning right, as an approaching driver will not be expecting a car to emerge from the fog in front of him.

If rear fog lamps are fitted to your car, use them when visibility is less than 100 metres but take care to switch them off when the weather improves. Many motorists forget to do this, sometimes motoring round for days dazzling all the drivers who are unfortunate enough to have to follow them.

Traffic

It is very easy to gain the impression in fog that a vehicle ahead of you is moving unnecessarily slowly; remember that while you can see a pair of red beacons through the fog, the driver ahead may be able to see virtually nothing. Never be tempted to overtake, since this invites a head-on collision with an oncoming vehicle. You can also be misled about visibility if you are following another vehicle, since its motion makes a slight 'hole' in the droplets of water vapour which form fog. You may feel that the fog has eased slightly while you are in another vehicle's wake, only to find, when you are committed to an overtaking manoeuvre, that it is as thick as ever.

While it is wise to stay in line, do not be tempted to stay in touch with the tail lights of a driver whose speed seems too fast for safety. In the sense of loneliness which accompanies fog it can be reassuring to drive in the presence of another vehicle, but do so only in a manner which is safe in the conditions. When you are following another vehicle, leave enough space to stop, remembering that the driver may not slow down and stop in the normal way. There is always the risk that the leader of a convoy will hit a crashed car and stop instantaneously. The result of nose-to-tail motoring can be catastrophic when a pile-up occurs, particularly on a motorway, but many people persist in driving too close and too fast despite constant pleas from the police and road safety bodies.

Publicity centres on motorway accidents in fog because they are so serious, but there is no reason why motorways should not be safer than other roads in fog, just as they are in normal weather conditions. Accidents would rarely occur if all drivers followed the rules outlined here instead of rushing blindly into the fog at high speed. You must look after yourself by driving safely and attentively if you find yourself being passed by these fools, and hope that a few may learn from your example. Illuminated motorway warning signals always post a temporary maximum speed when it is foggy, but follow your own judgement if you feel that the speed indicated is still too fast.

The dangers of fog can be reduced, although never eliminated, if you know what to expect. Listen to weather forecasts and traffic news on your car radio so that you are fully informed, and use your own experience to gauge how the weather is likely to develop during the course of your journey. Always remember that mist can occur in patches, sometimes when you least expect it. Pockets of fog can linger in valleys on an undulating country road, even in summer if the humidity, temperature and air currents are right; alternatively, high ground can be foggy on a very overcast day. Fog tends to form first over water; if you see mist developing, expect thicker patches where your road crosses a river.

You can imagine the danger if you are travelling at 60mph or so when you hit a patch of thick fog, so be prepared for it if you see any signs of mist over the surrounding landscape. Take all the usual precautions when mist does appear: drop your speed, switch on dipped headlights (and auxiliary fog lamps if you have them), and operate the windscreen wipers and washers frequently. Fog usually coats the windscreen with a thin film of moisture which gradually – and sometimes imperceptibly – reduces your visibility. Set the ventilation in the demist position to keep the windscreen clear, open the windows a little if it helps to reduce condensation inside the car, and switch on the heated rear window.

Summary

- The golden rule in fog is to *reduce your speed* so that you can stop within the *range of your vision*, even if this means that you drive at only 5mph.
- Always use *dipped headlights*, day or night.
- Take a sensible attitude in traffic: *do not overtake* because you may have been misled about the visibility while travelling behind another vehicle; do not stay in touch with a driver who is *travelling too fast*; always allow enough space so that you can stop safely if the vehicle ahead *stops instantaneously* in a collision.

21

ACCIDENTS

Every driver hopes never to be involved in an accident, but the chances of avoiding one throughout your motoring life are statistically quite small – even for an advanced driver. All the same, you are very likely sooner or later to arrive at the scene of an accident, and, if you are the first to arrive, it will be your responsibility to help. The advice which follows on what to do is from the Metropolitan Police.

Stop and think

Many things have to be done at once at an accident, and there is more involved than merely helping the casualties. You must warn other drivers, send for help and protect the site from further accidents until the emergency services arrive. your actions in these first few minutes could be a matter of life and death. Think about what you do: someone who is injured and unable to move could be more seriously hurt if you try to pull him out.

Park safely

Do not park your car where it could be a hazard to other drivers. The best place to park is at the roadside between the accident site and oncoming traffic where your car can be seen easily. Keep any children or pets inside the car. If it is dark, position your car so that its headlights illuminate the scene of the accident, but also so that it can still be seen by approaching drivers. Switch on your hazard warning lights. Switch off the crashed vehicle's engine and disconnect the battery; apply the handbrake and chock the wheels if this seems necessary. Make sure that no-one in the vicinity of the accident is smoking and if your car has a fire extinguisher keep it handy.

Warn other road users

Approaching drivers need plenty of time and distance in which to react to warning signals, and to slow down and stop or negotiate the accident. Running into the road and waving your arms wildly will confuse others and put yourself in danger. Instead, walk back along the side of the road for at least 100 yards, or until the accident is going out of view. Make a clear 'slow down' signal by moving your arm vigorously up and down, with palm face down, as if pressing down repeatedly on a heavy weight, and point decisively to the accident scene. On bends it may be useful to recruit a second person to give advance warning.

Someone should stand near the site and guide vehicles round the accident. Stand in the headlights of a car or under a streetlamp at night, and remember that it will help to wear a pale or reflective garment. Hold a white handkerchief, or better still a torch, in your hand to draw extra attention to yourself. If you carry an advance warning sign (a red reflective triangle), place it in the road at least 50 yards (150 yards on a motorway) before the accident and on the same side of the road to warn approaching traffic of the obstruction.

Send for help

Your first priority is to send for help, because you will need it! If this means leaving casualties unattended, get someone else to telephone the emergency services. If no-one else is around you must do this yourself.

Answer these questions

These questions must be answered before leaving the accident scene to telephone for the emergency services. What is the *exact* location? (Look for an obvious landmark if you do not know, or if there are no road signs.) How many casualties are there and how serious are their injuries? Are the casualties trapped? Is the accident causing danger? Is a traffic jam developing? Are petrol or chemicals spilling? How many vehicles are involved? Are they cars? Lorries? Tankers? Buses or coaches?

Dial 999

Tell the operator your telephone number and ask for ambulance, police or fire brigade; you will be connected to each in turn if all three are required. Ask for:

Ambulance if there are casualities.
Police if there are casualties, danger or obstruction to traffic.
Fire brigade if there are people trapped, petrol or chemicals on the road, or risk of fire.

Give this information

Details which should be given to the emergency services are: exact location of the accident; number and general condition of the casualties; if anyone is trapped; number and type of vehicles involved; if petrol or chemicals are on the road; if other traffic is in danger of jamming up; your name and address, and the telephone number from which you are speaking.

Then return to the accident scene to help with the casualties or traffic. If you saw what happened, give your name and address to the attending police officer. Try to avoid leaving the scene of the accident before speaking to the police but if you do, you should contact any police station or officer as soon as possible to give details.

If an accident occurs involving only slight damage to vehicles and no offence has been committed, it is not necessary to report it to the police. The drivers involved, however, are required by law to exchange details of driver, owner and vehicle registration number. If injury is caused you must also give your insurance particulars. Anyone requiring advice or assistance may telephone the local police station or, in an emergency, dial 999.

Help the casualties

Only move injured people if there is immediate danger, since you could aggravate internal and back or neck injuries. Make sure the person can breathe. Inspect the inside of the mouth and back of the throat. To avoid the danger of choking, remove any food, sweets or false teeth.

Listen, and if you cannot detect any breathing, try to restore the casualty by mouth-to-mouth resuscitation.

Place the casualty on his back, and support the neck so that the head falls back to open the airway. Pinch his nose shut and hold his mouth open. Cover his mouth with yours, and blow out firmly to inflate his lungs. Then release nose and mouth. Keep repeating the procedure until the casualty starts to breathe spontaneously. If he is unconscious, move him gently into the recovery position to make sure that he does not choke on his tongue or gorge. This involves turning the casualty gently on his side and bending his arms and legs so as to keep him in the position shown in the accompanying diagram. Straighten and turn his head to one side, facing slightly downwards.

If there is serious bleeding, apply firm pressure to the bleeding point to stem the flow of blood. Use a pad or apply a sterile dressing and bandage firmly. Look for limb fractures and try to stop these limbs moving. If a casualty is sitting up and in no immediate danger, do not make him leave the car. Leave him where he is and support his head in case he passes out and chokes.

Keep all casualties warm, including shock cases, but do not give them any pain relievers, alcohol, other drinks, food or cigarettes – they may have internal injuries and need operations.

If you are not sure what to do, leave well alone provided that the casualty is breathing and not bleeding heavily.

Get first aid training

This chapter gives only the most elementary first aid advice, but if you have been trained in first aid you will clearly be able to help more effectively. The British Red Cross Society or the St John Ambulance Association can advise you about training.

Carry a first aid kit

By carrying a first aid kit you are better prepared to help yourself and other road users in the event of an accident – it may even save someone's life. Your first aid kit should be

clearly marked and easily accessible, and can be carried in any suitable plastic container, preferably a flexible and transparent one. Mark it 'First Aid' or paint a large red cross on it.

This box should contain plenty of sterile dressings – as many as can be fitted in – in large, medium and small sizes. Triangular bandages for use as slings or bandages, safety pins, plasters, scissors and a knife are essential. You should carry anti-sting and scald ointments for minor mishaps which might impair your driving, but these should not be used in accidents. Do not carry antiseptics, pain-relieving pills or alcohol, as all of these can do more harm than good on the road.

(The Institute's thanks go to the Metropolitan Police for the above advice.)

Fire

There is just one set of circumstances at the scene of an accident when you should break the rule and pull injured people from their vehicles. Although fire occurs in only a tiny proportion of road accidents, it is a very serious hazard which requires instant action and great presence of mind. The fire may be caused by a short circuit from damaged wiring, in which case you should have plenty of time to deal with it as long as petrol is not seeping from a ruptured tank dangerously near it. If you have been wise enough to fit a fire extinguisher (ideally a 3lb-plus BCF model) to your car, aim it at the seat of the fire and keep up the discharge until the flames are out.

If the fire is in the engine bay, great care is needed since the action of opening the bonnet will feed the fire with a draught of air, causing the flames to flare up. If you can, open the bonnet just enough to allow you to aim the fire extinguisher inside, *but only if you can identify with certainty the source of the flames.* If you cannot see where the fire is coming from before you open the bonnet a

The recovery position (top, left) and the kiss of life. Their application is described above.

fraction, open it wide and be ready to act quickly if the fire expands. If you can, try to break the electrical circuit feeding the fire by disconnecting the battery leads.

A petrol fire is even more serious, calling for heroic action if anything is to be done to save people trapped inside the car. A petrol fire can often be avoided, however, by making sure that there is no possibility of any sparks near the damaged car: no-one must smoke, people in nailed shoes should keep clear and no attempt should be made by anyone but the emergency services to cut away metal to release occupants. Petrol cannot set itself alight, so one of your first actions must be to switch off the car's ignition to avoid the possibility of any sparks.

Accident procedures

The majority of accidents are no more than minor collisions involving bumps and scrapes to vehicles and no injury to people, but even these should be treated seriously. If you are involved in such an accident, the law demands that you give your name, address and insurance company details to the other driver, and to anyone else (such as a police officer) who may reasonably require it. It is your responsibility to make sure that you obtain these same details from the other driver. Remember to collect information from any other motorists or pedestrians who saw the incident, but be quick about it because witnesses, realising they might have to waste a day in court on your behalf, have a habit of melting away into the background.

You are not required by law to inform the police if all these points are followed, but it is always advisable to do so if anyone is injured or there is an allegation of dangerous driving. Many drivers think that causing damage to a parked vehicle is part of the rough and tumble of life, but it really is unethical to drive off without leaving a note of your name and address under the windscreen wiper.

Severe collisions

In collisions where more severe damage is caused to vehicles, it is best to leave them where they come to rest until the police have inspected the incident and taken measurements. Take photographs if you happen to be carrying a camera in your car, because they could be very useful as evidence if the matter ever comes before a court. Take your own measurements and make notes of exactly what happened so that you can give very precise information to your insurance company. The more detail you can provide, the better the chance, if the incident was the other driver's fault, that his company and not yours will be paying up.

Take care not to say anything, either to the other driver or to the police, which you may later regret. It is always possible that you may say things which may subsequently be interpreted as acceptance by you of liability. Think carefully before you speak even if you do accept that you were at fault; every insurer advises that you should leave the assessment of blame to them and not admit it on the spot.

Minor collisions

Very minor collisions, with only superficial damage to one or both cars, may cause a great deal of anger, but sometimes it is better to be philosophical if the incident is not your fault, and put the cost down to bad luck. On a busy road, other motorists will not thank you for causing a traffic jam while you argue over a broken tail lamp lens. The police also would not be pleased about being dragged into such an inconsequential matter which would hardly merit prosecution. You may be fortunate in finding that the other motorist agrees to pay for your minor repairs himself but, if he does not, you are unlikely to be able to persuade his insurance company to pay. They would know that the cost, time and trouble of legal action would never be worthwhile to extract a small amount of money, and you would hardly want to go to your own insurer with a claim which would probably be exceeded by the cost of higher premiums in the future. However annoying it may be at the time, you may have to put a minor knock down to experience.

'Hit and run' incidents

If ever you see a 'hit and run' accident, try to absorb as many details as you can and write them down as soon as possible: registration number, colour and make of the car involved, a description of the incident and maybe even a description of the driver. The more details you can pass to the police, the better chance they have of tracing the culprit. Do not forget, though, that your first duty is to the victim.

Summary

- Absorb carefully the details contained in this chapter about *accident procedure*; if you are one of the first on the scene you must act swiftly and with great presence of mind.
- Always carry a *first aid kit* and a *fire extinguisher* and make sure that you know how to use them.
- At minor accidents which involve no injury, your *exchange of details* with the other party should include names, addresses, vehicle details and names of insurance companies; do not admit liability even if you feel that you were at fault.

22

REACTION TIMES

As we saw in Chapter 6, a car travels a long way while its driver is simply reacting to a situation, and further still while the driver carries out his actions. While driving you must constantly allow for the reaction time needed before you brake, steer or accelerate when confronted by a hazard.

Your reactions

Reaction times vary widely from person to person, and are invariably longer than you might think. A professional racing driver who is physically fit, gifted in high speed driving and fired with adrenalin can react remarkably quickly, in as little as 0.2 of a second. This represents the time which elapses between the driver spotting a hazard and beginning his action, whether pressing the brake pedal, accelerating or moving the steering wheel. If you consider that it takes about one second to say 'one thousand', you begin to appreciate the lightning speed of a racing driver's reactions: in one-fifth of this time he can recognise a hazard, decide on the degree of danger, assess what might happen next, choose a course of action and than act on it.

The average motorist is much slower to react: around 0.5 of a second is still good, 0.8 of a second is satisfactory and even one second is not too bad. Anything longer than a second is beginning to be dangerously slow. You might have a rough idea, even an inflated one, of how good your reactions are, but your own time is difficult to measure unless you have a proper medically-verified check. Some driving centres have simulation testers: you sit at the simulated controls of a car and have to brake when a hazard, or just a 'brake' warning, flashes on the screen in front of you. There is also a party game which allows you to compare your reactions with those of other people simply by gripping a long piece of card which someone drops between your thumb and forefinger, but this is only a comparative guide.

Remember that the speed of your reactions can vary considerably; they slow down if you are tired, ill or under stress. If you have to drive when you are feeling at all below par, you must take this into account. Your reaction time might be 0.5 of a second when you are fit, but when you have a heavy cold it could increase to 0.8 of a second. That extra 0.3 of a second makes a tremendous difference to the distance you travel before you start to take avoiding action for a hazard ahead.

The accompanying tables show how far you travel for three different reaction times at various speeds. Assume that your reaction time approaches one second and allow for this in the semi-instinctive calculations you make on the road when judging braking distance, an overtaking manoeuvre and so on.

You should, of course, reduce the effect of your reaction time by reading the road and realising when and where a hazard might occur. If you suspect that potential danger lies ahead, it is always wise to lift off the accelerator and hold your right foot poised over the brake pedal. This anticipation will save valuable tenths of a second by eliminating the delay while the brain passes a 'lift off accelerator, move on to brake' message to your right foot.

You must allow more reaction time at night because your eyes have to adjust constantly to changing levels of light. The iris of the eye contracts quickly to adjust your vision when bright headlights approach, but it takes much longer to adapt to darkness again once the lights have gone; while your eyes adjust to the darkness you are driving with temporarily impaired vision. During these moments when it is more difficult to see what lies ahead, the time needed to recognise developments which may affect you will increase. Making allowance for this was discussed in Chapter 12; since your reaction time can rise to several seconds, reduce your speed accordingly.

The tables *below* show how far you travel in feet during every tenth of a second while reacting – and before operating the brakes or steering – for a quick reaction time of 0.4 seconds.

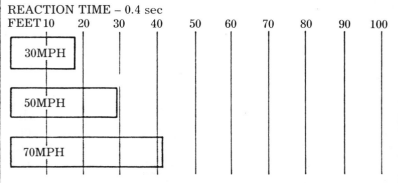

REACTION TIME – 0.4 sec

FEET	10	20	30	40	50	60	70	80	90	100
30MPH										
50MPH										
70MPH										

If you think these distances are suprisingly long, then look at table 2 (*below*), which is based on a reaction time of 0.7 seconds.

REACTION TIME – 0.7 sec

FEET	10	20	30	40	50	60	70	80	90	100
30MPH										
50MPH										
70MPH										

Alarming isn't it? But now look at table 3, calculated for a time of 0.9 seconds.

REACTION TIME – 0.9 sec

FEET	10	20	30	40	50	60	70	80	90	100
30MPH										
50MPH										
70MPH										

Other people's reactions

While you can take a little positive action to allow for the effect of your own reaction time, nothing can be done about the shortcomings of road users around you other than always to expect slow reactions in other drivers. It is common for someone involved in an accident to complain that the other driver 'had plenty of time to see me', and maybe by the aggrieved driver's standards he did. But sharp reactions in another driver cannot be taken for granted. An incident where two vehicles collide because Driver One pulls away too slowly across the path of Driver Two could be blamed on both parties; Driver Two is wrong to assume that Driver One has quick reactions and should allow room for his hesitant approach.

Before we leave the subject of reaction times, there are two popular myths which must be exploded. The first is the view, thankfully now rejected by the vast majority of drivers, that alcohol speeds up reactions. Drinking has precisely the *opposite* effect, for it dulls the nervous system so that you react more slowly to outside influences. The problem is that judgement diminishes under the influence of alcohol, so that some people *think* that they can react more quickly after a few drinks. It cannot be stressed too strongly that you should never drink and drive. Remember too that drugs can also slow you down, so when you are prescribed drugs ask your doctor if it is safe to drive. You should also read the labels on any pills you buy from a chemist; anti-sickness tables, for example, can have side-effects which are disastrous when you are driving.

The second myth is that familiar claim from drivers involved in an accident: 'I stopped dead'. Now that you know just how far you can travel while you are reacting to a hazard, you can see that this statement can never be true. Besides, no cars can ever stop 'dead': if they could, the occupants would be killed by the deceleration forces . . .

Summary

- Never underestimate your *reaction time*, or the distance your car can travel while you are reacting.

- Allow for the fact that your reaction time increases when you are *below par*: feeling unwell, sleepy or stressed can all affect your driving dramatically.
- Do not assume that *other drivers* will react as quickly as you expect them to.

23

IN GEAR

Skilled drivers know how to get the most from their cars when circumstances demand it, and an essential part of this ability is knowing how to make the best use of your car's gearbox. It is not enough to know how quickly your car accelerates when you press the pedal; you must also know what to expect in each gear and understand fully the proper use of the gearbox. Most cars have manual gearboxes with five – or sometimes four – forward gears, although many drivers opt for cars with various types of automatic transmission.

Using a manual gearbox

You must be sufficiently familiar with the gearbox to make any gear selection quickly, smoothly and accurately. The advanced test calls for an ability to go up and down the ratios; although today's all-synchromesh gearboxes reduce the problems, a degree of skill is still necessary.

Changing gear

When changing up a gear, you should release the accelerator completely and only press it again when the clutch has been re-engaged, timing these movements accurately so that you maintain smooth progress. When changing down a gear, however, you should keep a little pressure on the accelerator as you select the lower gear, so that the engine speed matches road speed when you engage the clutch. This technique, when perfected, gives a very smooth change and puts less strain on the transmission. When executed with finesse, all up and down gearchanges should be so smooth that your passengers do not notice them.

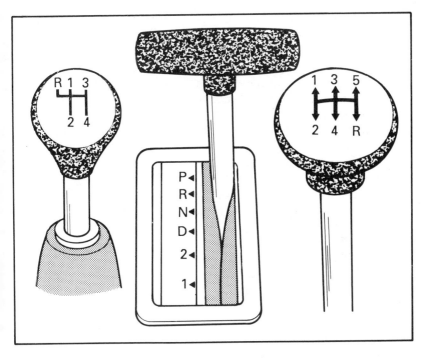

Some common types of gear selection levers. On the left is a typical gear lever for a four-speed manually operated gearbox. On the right is its five-speed counterpart. The central stick is typical of any automatics, and the letters indicate parking lock (P), which locks the transmission when the car is stationary (a useful adjunct to the handbrake); reverse (R); neutral (N) – note that you must usually select P or N in order to allow the engine to be started; forward drive (D) – this can be selected and left alone for most purposes; and low gears (1 or 2), which are for holding the car in that particular gear.

Double de-clutching

This is a more difficult technique which all drivers once used to have to master to cope with non-synchromesh gearboxes. Although it has little relevance these days, it is worth describing the double-declutching procedure in case you ever have to drive a car without synchromesh on first gear, or even a classic car with no synchromesh at all. When changing up a gear, depress the clutch pedal and release the accelerator, move the gear lever into neutral, let up the clutch for a moment and then push it down again and engage the gear. When changing down a gear, depress the clutch pedal and move the gear lever into neutral; bring up the clutch pedal while in neutral and rev the engine to synchronise speed with the lower gear; finally depress the clutch again and engage the gear. This takes a good deal of practice to co-ordinate what seems a complicated operation and to acquire a feel for the necessary engine speed, but eventually double-declutching will become second nature – a premise which applies to so many aspects of good driving. Some drivers double-declutch when using a modern gearbox, but there is really no point as synchromesh does the job for you.

Correct usage

Correct use of the gears is one of the basics of advanced driving. You should always move. away from standstill in first gear even if the car is capable of doing it in second. Starting in second wears out the clutch more quickly because you have to engage it more slowly and let it slip more; furthermore, your initial acceleration is less urgent and there is a greater risk of stalling the engine.

You need to know the maximum speeds (up to 70mph) which your car can manage in each intermediate gear. These are often marked with a tiny stroke on the car's speedometer or listed in the manufacturer's handbook. Never hesitate to take your car to these speeds if it is necessary when overtaking, but take care not to extend the engine beyond these limits. Do not attempt to change down a gear if this means that you will exceed the maximum for that gear.

Rev counter

An increasing number of relatively modest cars are now fitted with a rev counter, which shows the engine speed in revolutions per minute (20 = 2000rpm, 30 = 3000rpm and so on). This is a very useful instrument, despite the fact that incompetent drivers have been known to confuse it with the speedometer. Most rev counters are marked with an orange sector to warn when you are approaching the engine's limit, and a red sector to indicate that limit; memorise the limit if it is not indicated in this way. As well as showing you the engine's limit, a rev counter can also be useful in making the most of your engine's power characteristics. For example, if you sense that the engine pulls most strongly between 3500rpm and 5000rpm, the rev counter can help you to decide the gear you need to make best use of this rev band for overtaking. The rev counter is also a useful guide for ensuring that you do not labour the engine by asking it to pull strongly from low revs; although you should be able to recognise the sound of an engine beginning to struggle, the rev counter is a source of extra information. Few engines provide much acceleration below 2000rpm, so you should keep above this speed for smooth performance.

Which gear?
You should strike a balance between economy, performance and mechanical sympathy when choosing which gear to be in. Some drivers seem determined to remain in top gear for as long as possible, while others hold intermediate gears for so long that the engine races away at high revs: your approach should be the sensible one, between these extremes. You should make the fullest use of the gearbox for occasions when a lower gear would be better, such as when overtaking or climbing hills; a low gear should always be used for maximum engine braking when going down a steep hill. At the same time, avoid changing gear more often than necessary, since modern engines are fairly flexible.

Gears or brakes?
Many drivers have been brought up to believe that they should use the gears to help slow down the car by going down through the gearbox, gear by gear, when approaching a roundabout or junction. This may once have been advisable when car braking systems were primitive, but on today's cars it is an unnecessary complication (unless you have to contend with brake failure) which will shorten the life of your clutch and gearbox. After all, a set of brake pads is a fraction of the cost of a new gearbox. You should slow down with the brakes and select the gear you need as the speed drops: approaching a roundabout, for example, you might 'block'

change directly from fifth to third, if this is the gear appropriate for accelerating again.

Using automatic transmission

Automatic transmissions remove all these decisions because they can think for themselves. Conventional automatics have three or four forward speeds and can be left with the selector in position 'D' (for drive). They will change up and down automatically as well as providing the clutch action to move you away from rest and to disengage the drive when the car stops again. When more brisk acceleration is required, perhaps for overtaking or gaining speed on a motorway slip road, the 'kickdown' facility provides it by engaging a suitable lower gear when you push the accelerator down fully.

Occasions do arise when the driver's judgement is superior to that of the automatic transmission, so 'hold' positions for the intermediate ratios are available on the selector. If you want maximum acceleration right to the engine's limit, it can be better to control the selector yourself to avoid the slight pause in your progress produced by an automatic change.

A car with automatic transmission will usually creep forward with the selector at 'D' even if you remove your foot from the accelerator, so put the selector in neutral and apply the handbrake when you expect to be stopped for more than a few seconds. If you are stopped only momentarily, perhaps when joining a queue which is just about to move off, you can simply hold the car on the brake pedal until it is clear to move again.

A few cars are fitted with a different type of automatic transmission which involves simply selecting whether you want to go forwards or backwards. The familiar 'elastic band' Variamatic transmission used in DAFs and the related Volvo 66 (both of which are quite old cars now) relies on steel-reinforced flexible belts running over expanding pulleys to provide an infinitely variable range of ratios. The theory was good, but reliability doubts – centred on problems with stretched belts – prevented the Variamatic becoming more widely adopted. A more recent development of this principle is the Continuously Variable

Transmission (CVT) pioneered by Ford and Fiat. This uses a well-engineered multi-link steel belt which passes over two pulleys: when the accelerator is depressed, the drive pulley closes progressively as the driven pulley opens, giving a stepless transmission. The selector is placed in 'Drive' when you are moving but has a 'Low' setting for maximum acceleration or stronger engine braking down hills.

Although no gearbox – manual or automatic – should be used in place of the brakes, both can be used to help in the process of slowing down if necessary in an emergency. Remember, though, that engine braking is less effective with an automatic than a manual. An automatic will seem strange when you first handle one, if you have become accustomed to a manual, so be very cautious until you are used to it. Never use your left foot on the brake just because it has no other role.

If you passed your driving test in a car fitted with automatic transmission, you will be restricted to driving cars of this type, which could be a great handicap one day. You should take another test at the earliest opportunity in a car with a manual gearbox to obtain a full licence to drive any car. It is also worth pointing out that some automatics can be damaged if the car is towed after a breakdown. Always check in the manufacturer's handbook about the advisability of towing.

Summary

- Gear changes should be made so *smoothly and precisely* that passengers do not notice them; smooth downward changes require a little pressure on the accelerator to match engine speed to road speed when drive takes up again.
- *Correct use of the gears* is a basic requirement of advanced driving; use the intermediate ratios whenever they are necessary, including for strong acceleration.
- Do not go down *through the gears* to slow down the car, except in an emergency: the brakes do this job.

However, use a low gear for maximum engine braking down a steep hill.

- *Automatic gearboxes* remove most of this decision making, but do consider using intermediate ratio 'hold' positions when crisp acceleration is needed.

SYMPATHY AND UNDERSTANDING

A basic understanding of what goes on under the bonnet as you drive will give you a greater appreciation of your car, and may even help you to drive it more sensitively. After all, if you treat your car properly it will serve you better. A car is an elaborate machine designed to transport you and your passengers; you, as the operator, can control it more effectively if you know how it works. It is beyond the brief of this book to explore the engineering of a car in great detail, but there are many publications on the subject suitable for everyone from interested layman to qualified engineer. If you count yourself as one of the former, an elementary description of how a car works might be helpful.

Understanding how a car works

The internal combustion engine works by burning petrol or diesel fuel with a mixture of air to create an expansion of gas which drives the pistons. These pistons drive a rotating shaft, called a crankshaft, which is connected to the gearbox by a clutch. The clutch can be released so that the engine can run while the car is standing still. A Wankel rotary engine effectively has its rotating shaft profiled to create a rotor which is driven by the expanding gases.

The gearbox contains combinations of gearwheels which give the various ratios as they are selected by the driver. A gearbox is necessary so that the engine can run within its comfortable speed range (normally about 2000rpm to 6000rpm) regardless of road speed. You start in first gear and change up as speed increases. Power is taken to the driven wheels (which may be at either the front or back, or both on a four-wheel drive car) by means of articulated shafts.

The car is suspended on its wheels by pivoted arms which allow the movement necessary over the undulations of the road surface. The springs, either of the coil or leaf type, insulate the car and its occupants from bumps and hollows in the road surface, and shock absorbers prevent the springs from continuing to oscillate after they are compressed and released again. Springs and shock absorbers also act to keep the wheels and tyres firmly in contact with the road.

The brakes consist of special high-friction pads which are pressed against each side of a disc or the inner face of a drum to slow down the rotation of the wheel. The driver's movement on the brake pedal increases the pressure in the hydraulic actuating system so that the brakes are made to grip the discs or drums with great force.

People with a good understanding of a car's engineering will hopefully forgive this most basic summary, but it may help some readers who have always preferred not to worry about what goes on under the bonnet.

Sympathy with your car

A good driver never abuses his engine by asking it to pull above or below its normal operating range. Large engines (perhaps with six, eight or even twelve cylinders) can run quite happily down to virtual tickover speed, and highly tuned engines can rev higher than the average, but between 2000rpm and 6000rpm is the approximate range for a typical four-cylinder engine. A good driver does not attempt to engage top gear much below 2000rpm, nor does he rev his engine constantly to its limit. He uses the gearbox so that his engine is always running comfortably, which means using only part throttle once he has reached a reasonable cruising speed. It is quite wrong to drive unnecessarily quickly and be forced to jam on the brakes at every obstacle. You should always drive at a 'happy balance' speed, and err on the slow side rather than the fast.

The clutch is invariably the most abused mechanical part of a car, and for many drivers it is the first major component to fail as the miles clock up. As the device responsible for transmitting the engine's power to the gearbox, the clutch comprises two facing discs with a mechanism which brings them together to engage drive or pulls them apart to release it. A lining of friction material provides the grip, so it is easy to see how slipping the clutch causes this lining to wear out more quickly. A clutch can last for 100,000 miles or more if it is treated with respect, yet a driver with no mechanical sympathy can ruin one within 5000 miles.

A driver who uses the clutch pedal as a rest for his left foot (and there are plenty!) will have to pay for many new clutches throughout his motoring life, yet may never realise that he is at fault. He might think that the slight pressure of a foot resting lightly on the pedal causes no harm, but it is just enough to let the clutch slip a little all the time, which wears it out quickly. Some lazy drivers also use the clutch to hold the car on a hill, balancing the clutch's biting point against engine revs so that the car remains stationary. It is far safer, and in the long run cheaper, to use the handbrake, as you were taught to do for the Government driving test.

Another fault which can develop, without a driver realising it, is to use the clutch pedal to control the speed of the car. He might dip the clutch to lose a little speed when negotiating a corner, then feed it in gently for the next straight stretch of road. The thinking seems to be that this tactic avoids the need to change down a gear, but the effect is to wear out the clutch and leave the driver in the wrong gear for the conditions.

Slipping the clutch occurs when it is released too gently, but it is also possible to use it too sharply. Frequent 'jack rabbit' starts can cause all sorts of expensive damage to your car. They strain the entire transmission system as well as the engine (causing gearbox breakage in extreme cases), wear out the tyres and damage the universal joints in the drive shafts, this last fault being recognised by a loud 'clonk' every time you change gear.

The need for mechanical sympathy also extends to the gearbox. Any 'graunching' always results in wear to gearwheel teeth, or even broken teeth, so take care to disengage the clutch fully before changing gear and push the gear lever fully home before releasing the clutch again. Trying to change gear in too much of a hurry is the cause; the worst 'graunching' occurs when a driver attempts to select reverse gear too quickly after rolling to a standstill, or even an instant before the car has stopped.

Every component on your car benefits from careful treatment, including the brakes. Leaving your braking to the last moment is not only risky, but also wears out the pads and tyres more quickly. New tyres amount to a significant proportion of the cost of running a car, so remember that mechanical sympathy – an essential part of advanced driving – extends to these too.

Summary

- If you do not know how a car works, acquire at least a *basic mechanical understanding* so that you are better equipped to treat it properly.
- Drive with *mechanical sympathy*: do not extend the *engine* below or above its reasonable operating range; treat the *clutch* with respect; and avoid causing a 'graunching' sound in the *gearbox* by changing gear too hastily.

25

TOWING

So many drivers tow trailers of one kind or another – platforms for boats, horses or racing cars, as well as caravans – that the Institute of Advanced Motorists operates a special towing test. Only existing members who have already passed the advanced test in a car or commercial vehicle are eligible. The basic points to remember when towing a trailer are these:

- Keep the nose weight on the trailer fairly high but not excessive: a downward force of between 50lb and 150lb is usually needed to ensure stability.
- Always double-check that the tow-ball is fully latched home, that safety chains and emergency brake pulls are in position and that all lights on the trailer (which must carry your vehicle's registration number) are working.
- Ensure that any load is properly secured.
- Check tyre pressures on your vehicle and the trailer: pressures in the rear tyres of the towing vehicle may need to be increased, and pressures in the trailer's tyres must be at the manufacturer's recommended level – which may be considerably higher than the tow vehicle's pressures.
- Release the parking brake and any overrun brake catch on the trailer's drawbar.

Braking

You will find that the extra weight, perhaps a ton or more, of a laden trailer will create so much added momentum that stopping distances increase considerably, even if the trailer has overrun brakes. On a long motorway journey with a very stable trailer, never allow yourself to forget temporarily that you are towing, so that you find yourself

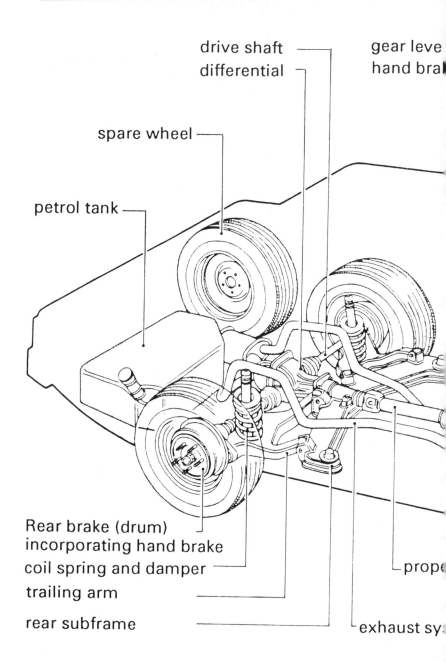

drive shaft

differential

gear leve

hand bra

spare wheel

petrol tank

Rear brake (drum)
incorporating hand brake

coil spring and damper

trailing arm

rear subframe

prop

exhaust sy

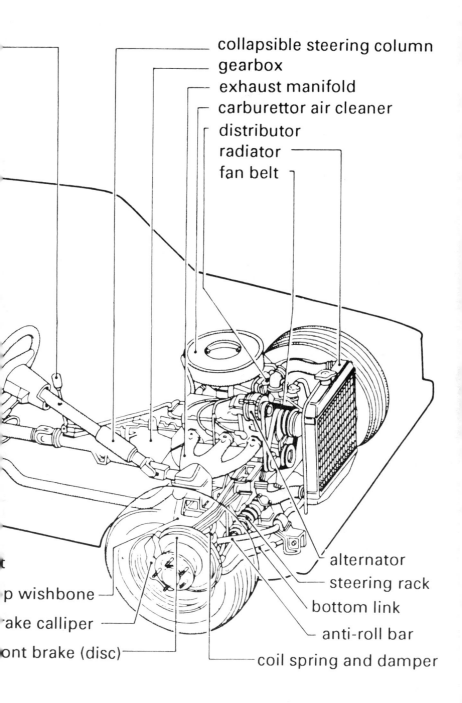

collapsible steering column
gearbox
exhaust manifold
carburettor air cleaner
distributor
radiator
fan belt

alternator
steering rack
bottom link
anti-roll bar
coil spring and damper

p wishbone
ake calliper
ont brake (disc)

in the position of having to brake very heavily for a roundabout at the end of an exit slip road.

In traffic

It is vital to allow for the extra width of a trailer, and to remember that the trailer will cut in closer to the kerb than the car itself when negotiating junctions or sharp bends. If it is safe to do so, make a larger arc; alternatively, copy the technique used by drivers of articulated lorries by drawing slightly past the apex of the junction with the 'tractor unit' (your car), then turn the corner sharply.

Rear vision

If you are towing anything other than a flat trailer, the mirrors on your car will be useless. It is essential, therefore, to buy mirrors on extended arms to give yourself adequate rearward vision.

Legal requirements

The law affecting the use of trailers is too complex for all the details to be given here, so check by asking the local police or the company which supplies your trailer. Speed limits vary considerably according to the road and the design of the trailer, and no trailer may be used in lane 3 of a motorway. In addition, there are requirements governing lights, rear reflectors and the display of 50mph warning signs at the rear.

Although it is not a legal requirement, we would recommend that you fit sidelights on a trailer's mudguards; they should show white to the front and red to the rear. This precaution could prevent an accident since other road users frequently fail to see a trailer, particularly if it is unladen.

Manoeuvring

Reversing is what sorts the men from the boys as far as trailers are concerned. It is so tricky when you first attempt it that you would be wise to practise in a wide open

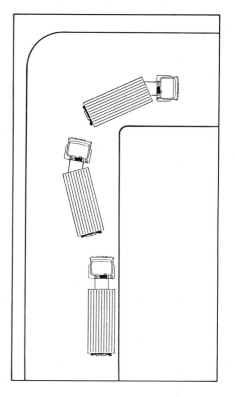

Reversing a trailer. If you wish to make the trailer swing to the left you must begin by reversing to the right; when the trailer has started to line up in the required direction, correct the steering and start backing to the left. Always reverse very slowly.

space, perhaps in a public car park on a Sunday morning, before you have to do it in tight confines. As soon as you have a go, you will find that the trailer will travel in the opposite direction to that in which the car is heading: if you back round to the left, the trailer will veer to the right.

Overcoming this requires a special technique. If you wish to make the trailer swing to the left, you must begin by reversing to the right; when the trailer has started to line up in the required direction, correct the steering and start backing to the left. Just like any other aspect of driving it takes a little time to master this, but once you have acquired the knack it will seem easy. Always reverse very slowly because any mistake will be quickly compounded as the trailer moves rapidly off course; edge forward and have another go if necessary. In an extreme case it is possible to apply so much steering lock that the trailer jack-knifes and becomes jammed against the towing car's rear bumper. Remember that you may need to latch overrun brakes out of use if they are not to become clamped on as soon as you reverse.

One of the biggest dangers on the open road is the dreaded swing. Many trailers and caravans are prone at certain speeds to begin oscillating from side to side, creating a pendulum effect which produces greater and greater swings until car and trailer are in danger of catapulting themselves off the road – or into another vehicle. Your only course of action is to slow down gently, but make sure that it *is* gently because heavy braking could launch the unsteady trailer into even more violent swings. Stop as soon as possible in order to adjust the weight on the trailer so that more weight bears down on the drawbar.

Summary

- If you need to drive with a trailer or caravan, take the special *towing test* run by the Institute of Advanced Motorists.
- Allow a much greater *stopping distance* when towing a trailer.
- You are bound by different *legal requirements* when towing: make sure you understand how the law applies to your use of a trailer or caravan.
- Practise in an open space in order to learn the knack of *reversing a trailer.*

26

DRIVING ABROAD

Twenty-five years ago it was considered quite adventurous for a British driver to take his car on holiday on the continent, but nowadays over a third of Britain's motorists have experienced the pleasures of driving abroad. If you keep off the busy trunk roads, autoroutes, autostradas and autobahns, you can follow quiet highways which carry much less traffic than you usually find on our crowded island. There is no reason why a competent driver should not feel perfectly confident when driving in an unfamiliar country, on the 'wrong' side of the road. Even busy cities such as Paris and Rome – with their reputation for devil-may-care traffic – should hold no fears as long as you follow the basic rules of advanced driving.

Planning ahead

Just like any other aspect of advanced driving, you should plan ahead to make the most of a continental holiday, or even a business trip. When you have decided on your destination, buy the appropriate large-scale road maps from any good bookshop. The Michelin series, which cover the whole of Europe, are among the best, and these are also now available as high-quality atlases of France or Europe, published by Hamlyn. If you are in a hurry you may be forced to use motorways, but remember that tolls are charged to use those in France, Switzerland and Italy. If you have time, it is much more enjoyable to plan a leisurely journey on quieter roads.

A good way of planning a route is to draw a pencil line on the map between your ferry arrival port and your destination, and then ink in a route along roads – choosing plenty of secondary roads if your journey time allows it – running close to the pencil line. Your passengers will need to play their part in navigation, but this can add to the pleasure of the journey for them. Choosing smaller roads will force you to allow more time for the trip, but it will provide a delightful and more relaxing way to see the country, and your passengers will certainly appreciate driving through a more attractive landscape.

In addition to maps, you will need guide books to tell you about places of interest and where to stay, but make use also of the free brochures and leaflets which the tourist information centres in most large continental towns can provide. You may even be able to obtain useful information before you leave on your holiday by contacting the London office of the appropriate national tourist board.

RAC or AA members can make travel arrangements through these organisations, which offer particularly good insurance packages to take care of your car's return to Britain if you are unlucky enough to suffer a major breakdown. It would be worth taking out insurance to cover health care and theft, no matter how remote these possibilities may seem. As far as normal car insurance is concerned, you should tell your insurer or broker where you are going and arrange a Green Card. Your normal insurance arrangements (fully comprehensive if you have any sense) should be extended to cover you while you are abroad. Extra cover is not legally required when travelling in EC countries, but the basic cover provided automatically is a bare minimum. You will have enough to worry about in the unfortunate event of an accident or breakdown abroad without having the extra headache of the cost.

Differences to watch for

The moment when you drive off the ferry and into another country is always exciting. At first you will keep reminding yourself to drive on the right, and multi-lingual warning signs along the road leaving the ferry terminal will reinforce your awareness. This should ensure that you get used to driving on the correct side of the road without mishap for the first few miles; but the trouble can come later when you have gained some experience and feel more confident. It is all too easy, when there is no traffic to remind you, to forget momentarily that you must drive on the 'wrong' side of the road. The time to be on your guard is whenever you stop the car, particularly if you do so on the left-hand side of the road. It may seem quite natural to come out of a shop or filling station, get in the car and set off up the road on the *left*.

Apart from the self-evident fact that you drive on the other side, most continental traffic rules are the same as British ones – with one important exception which we shall examine in a moment. Traffic signs present no worries because Britain long ago adopted the international pattern, and you can decipher the few local pecularities by using common sense and a little imagination. In France, you might see a red warning triangle sign bearing the silhouette of a frog: yes, it means that you must beware of frogs on the road, because the surface will be slippery if large numbers have been squashed by traffic.

You need to be extra careful in spotting traffic lights because they are often suspended from overhead cables, with a small 'reminder' set at eye level to the right for the driver first in a queue. In some countries the amber intermediate stage is omitted, and you tend to find far more filter systems (for left, right and straight on). A continuously flashing amber light is frequently used, but need cause no confusion: it simply means that you should cross a particularly hazardous junction with great caution and be prepared to give way. If you drive in a large Italian city, be prepared for the drivers you see making their own 'filtering' decisions at lights by nipping round a corner at red when no traffic is coming. This would rightly be regarded as a serious offence at home, but strangely the Italian authorities seem almost to accept it as an initiative which, if done safely, gets traffic flowing that little bit more freely.

The important exception to British traffic rules mentioned earlier is the notorious 'priority to the right' rule, seen at its most virulent in France. Thankfully, the French authorities, motivated by having one of the highest road accident rates in Europe, are at last trying to sort out the dangers of their 'priority to the right' policy, but you must still be on your guard. Roundabouts can cause confusion because the traditional French system is the opposite to ours, meaning that traffic on the roundabout must give way to traffic coming in at each entrance road. All this is in the process of changing, with many roundabouts now having white lines to indicate that incoming traffic must give way in the normal manner, but always be prepared to find the old system operating.

The same wisdom applies to traffic in towns or on country roads. It has always been necessary in France to expect a *Deux Chevaux* to come hurtling into your path from any side road to the right. Although better use of white line 'give way' markings is now being made to establish a more logical system of priority, you will still find local drivers joining a major road from the right without even slowing down or looking to see if it is clear, trusting to luck that any oncoming drivers will be able to give way. You need to be especially cautious in towns, because 'priority to the right' applies at any junction without traffic lights or 'give way' road markings. Only when travelling along a major road dotted with yellow diamond 'you have priority' signs can you be reasonably sure that a car will not emerge from a side road to the right.

In addition to this warning, there are a few other aspects of continental motoring which require special care. These are mentioned to help you enjoy your European touring holiday, and not with the aim of putting you off.

Continental policemen, especially the motorcycle police in France, tend to take a much harder line with erring motorists than their British counterparts. They will listen to no excuses about ignorance of the law in their country, and invariably they will deal with a misdemeanour committed by a British motorist in the simplest way – by demanding an on-the-spot fine. Their system is well organised, with all major credit cards accepted! Make sure that you understand the speed limits in each country you enter, because a speeding offence is the most common reason for a British driver being stopped. There is one important point about driving on German autobahns: although they are the only motorways in Europe without an overall speed limit, 100kph (60mph) and 120kph (75mph) limits *are* often posted for short stretches, sometimes for no obvious reason. They can appear by surprise, but take note of how rigidly German motorists obey them; the fines for not doing so are heavy.

Although petrol of a grade equivalent to four-star can be found everywhere in Europe these days (except perhaps behind the Iron Curtain), make sure that you understand the local description for the grade you require. Be especially careful that you do not unwittingly fill up at an unleaded pump when you need leaded fuel (or vice versa) simply because you do not understand the language.

The yellow headlights fitted to French cars are required by law on all French-registered vehicles, but visitors may use their ordinary white lights. Before heading to any country, however, you must have the right-hand bias of your dipped beam masked by fitting the adhesive shapes available from accessory shops. Do this even if you do not expect to be driving in darkness, because even the best-laid plans can go wrong. If you neglect to do this, you will find yourself 'flashed' by dazzled oncoming drivers because your dipped headlights will look as if they are on main beam.

Apart from this point, your car needs no more preparation than it requires for any other long journey. Make sure the list of European dealers supplied when the car was new is still in your glovebox, and try to obtain a phrase book which lists common motoring terms if you will be struggling with language in the event of a breakdown. Have your car serviced before you leave if one will be due while you are away. Although a red warning triangle is recommended for use in Britain, you *must* take one when travelling abroad. It is a good idea to take some basic spares, such as lamp bulbs, fuses and a fan or alternator belt, as well as a plastic emergency windscreen. And finally, remember your GB plate!

Summary

- *Plan ahead* as far as possible so that you have a good idea of your route before you leave home.
- Once your initial wariness about *driving on the right* has disappeared, it is easy to forget momentarily that you are abroad; be especially careful not to drive

away on the left after a short stop at a filling station or shop.

- Always be alert to the dangers of the *'priority to the right'* rule when driving in France.
- Use common sense and imagination to decipher any *unfamiliar road signs*; make sure you know the *speed limits* for the countries you visit.
- Do not think that *ignorance of the law* will ever be accepted as an excuse by continental policemen.

27

NOW FOR THE TEST

Now that you have absorbed all the advice in this book, if you are not already a member of the Institute of Advanced Motorists you must be wondering whether you have developed the ability to pass the advanced driving test.

Just how good a driver are you? Very expert, you may think, but are you sure? You must remember that the Government driving test is only a very basic, elementary examination; the real learning starts when you can throw away your L-plates. Passing the ordinary driving test, even if you did so with ease at your first attempt, is only a starting point in the acquisition of mature driving skills. Fortunately, most drivers realise this and there comes a time when they want to reassure themselves that their skill is developing along the right lines.

This is why the Institute of Advanced Motorists exists. It was founded in 1956 as a non-profit making organisation and is registered as a charity. It is dedicated to the promotion of road safety by encouraging motorists to take pride in good driving. By taking the IAM's test, drivers can measure the progress they have made since passing their basic driving test.

The advanced driving test

The test lasts for about 90 minutes and is something which any driver of reasonable experience and skill should be able to pass without difficulty. Whether candidates pass or fail, however, they all learn a great deal from the Class One police drivers who act as the examiners on test routes located all over Britain.

Skill with responsibility – this is what the IAM aims to promote. The number of road accidents (there are over 300,000 casualties and over 5000 deaths every year) would decrease dramatically if every driver had the ability to pass the IAM test and the self-discipline to adhere to its standards at all times. You have to pass the test to become a member of the IAM.

The IAM was founded by motorists from all walks of life with the common aim of making our roads safer by raising driving standards. It is controlled by a Council whose members are elected as a result of their expertise in various spheres of motoring. They represent accident prevention authorities, medicine, the motor industry and trade, the police, driving schools, magistrates, the motoring press, other motoring organisations and the IAM's own area Groups.

Ever since it started, the IAM's activities have been endorsed by successive Transport Ministers. As an expert organisation, its opinions on road safety issues are regularly sought by the Government. Indeed, one of its main aims is to represent the views of skilled, responsible motorists to the authorities; each new member, therefore, becomes a valuable addition to the campaign for better driving and safer roads.

So far, some 300,000 motorists have taken the advanced driving test and 70 per cent of them have passed and become members of the IAM. Of these successful drivers, one in five is a woman; men and women have similar success rates in the test. The Army has adopted the test at home and abroad, and more than 350 companies use it as a stringent check on the driving skills of staff using company-owned vehicles.

What does the test involve?

A typical test route covers around 35–40 miles and incorporates all kinds of road conditions, including congested urban areas, main roads, narrow country lanes and residential streets. You are not expected to give a display of fancy driving. On the contrary, you should handle your car in the steady, workmanlike way in which you should drive every day. The examiners do not, for example, expect exaggeratedly slow speeds or excessive signalling. They do want to see candidates drive with due regard for road, traffic and weather conditions, and all speed limits must be observed. They will want to see you driving briskly and to ensure that you are not afraid to cruise at the legal limit when circumstances permit – progress with safety.

You will be asked to carry out certain manoeuvres. You will need to reverse round a corner, reverse and park, turn in the road using forward and reverse gears, and make a hill start. There will be one or two spot checks on your powers of observation. There are no trick questions in the test and no attempts to catch you out. You are no longer required to give a running commentary at any time, although you are free to do so if you wish to make extra clear your ability to 'read the road'.

Who can take the test?

Anyone with a full British or EC driving licence, provided that he has not been convicted of a serious traffic offence in the last three years. You can take the test in almost any car which you provide yourself, in most vans and trucks, and certain three-wheelers.

How about disabled drivers?

Disabled drivers are welcome as candidates provided that they use a suitably adapted car.

Where can the test be taken?

Almost certainly quite near your home. The IAM has a nationwide network of test routes, as you will see from the list on page 182. The examiner will meet you at a pre-arranged rendezvous. Tests are available from Monday to Friday.

Can the driver prepare?

Yes, of course. This book covers all the ground you need to be familiar with to become an advanced driver, but many other manuals are also available. Some professional driving instructors *may* coach pupils up to the standard of the advanced test. In addition, you can ask your local council's road safety officer for details of advanced driving courses in your area, and in many areas the IAM's own local groups (details from the IAM, see page 181) can help you to prepare through their Associate Group Member Schemes.

Who are the examiners?

They are all holders of the Class One Police driving certificate. This means that they have passed the stiffest test of driving ability in Britain – the Police examination for traffic patrol drivers.

Here in greater detail are some of the points the examiners look for and comment on in their test reports:

Acceleration
Smooth and progressive? Excessive or insufficient? Is acceleration used at the right time and place?

Braking
Smooth and progressive or late and fierce? Are the brakes used in conjunction with mirror and signals? Are road, traffic and weather conditions taken into account?

Clutch control
Are engine and road speeds properly co-ordinated when changing gear? Does the candidate slip or ride the clutch? Does he coast with the clutch disengaged?

Gear changing
Is it a smooth change action, without jerking? If automatic transmission is fitted, does the driver make full use of it?

Use of gears
Are the gears correctly selected and used? Is the right gear selected before reaching a hazard?

Steering
Is the wheel held correctly with the hands at the quarter-to-three or ten-to-two positions? Does the driver pass the wheel through his hands? (Use of the 'cross arms' technique, except when manoeuvring in confined spaces, is not recommended.)

Driving position
Is the candidate alert or does he slump at the wheel? Does he nonchalantly rest an arm on the door while driving?

Observation
Does he 'read' the road ahead and show a good sense of anticipation? Does he show the ability to judge speed and distance?

Concentration
Does the driver keep his attention on the road? Does he allow himself to be distracted easily?

Maintaining progress
Bearing in mind the road, traffic and weather conditions, does the driver keep up a reasonable pace and maintain good progress?

Obstruction
Is the candidate careful not to obstruct other vehicles, by driving too slowly, taking up the wrong position on the road, or failing to anticipate and react correctly to the traffic situation ahead?

Positioning
Does the driver keep to the correct part of the road, especially when approaching or negotiating hazards?

Lane discipline
Does the candidate keep to the appropriate lane? Is he careful not to straddle white lines?

Observation of road surfaces
Does the driver keep an eye on the road surface,

especially in bad weather, and does he watch out for slippery conditions?

Traffic signals
Are signals, signs and road markings observed, obeyed and approached correctly? Does the driver show courtesy at pedestrian crossings?

Speed limits and other legal requirements
Are they observed? (The examiner cannot condone breaches of the law.)

Overtaking
Is this carried out safely and decisively, maintaining the right distance from other vehicles and using the mirror, signals and gears correctly?

Hazard procedure and cornering
Are road and traffic hazards coped with properly? Are bends and corners taken in the right manner?

Mirror
Does the candidate frequently use the mirror? Does he use it in conjunction with his signals and before changing speed or course?

Signals
Are turn indicator signals – and hand ones when needed – given at the right place and in good time? Are the horn and headlight flasher used in accordance with the *Highway Code*?

Restraint
Does the candidate show reasonable restraint – but not indecision – at the wheel?

Consideration
Is sufficient consideration and courtesy shown to other road users?

Car sympathy
Does the driver treat the car with care? Does he overstress

it, perhaps by revving the engine needlessly or by fierce braking?

Manoeuvring
Finally, are manoeuvres, such as reversing, performed smoothly and competently?

Results

At the end of your test your examiner will, after announcing your result, give an expert view of your skill and responsibility at the wheel. There may be praise, and certainly constructive criticism will be offered – the IAM aims to be entirely honest with you. Occasionally, a candidate is found to have developed a potentially dangerous fault of which he is completely unaware; a quiet word from the examiner will help him to correct it. You will not be failed for minor faults.

When you pass

When you pass the advanced test and become a member of the IAM, these are among the benefits available to you:

- *Badge*: The right to display the IAM's badge on your car, providing visible proof of the standard you have set yourself.
- *Insurance*: An introduction to motor insurers who may give special terms, subject to a satisfactory proposal.
- *RAC concessionary rates*: Special discounts, which have been negotiated by the IAM, for the range of rescue, recovery and home start services offered by the RAC.
- *Magazine*: A motoring magazine, *Milestones*, which is published every four months; it is produced specially for IAM members and written by and for people who take a keen interest in driving and cars.
- *Social activities*: The chance to meet other men and women who share your outlook on motoring. You can decide to join one of the IAM's local groups and take

part in the road safety driving and social events which they organise.

The Institute of Advanced Motorists is based at IAM House, 359 Chiswick High Road, London W4 4HS; telephone 01–994 4403 (24-hour answering service).

LIST OF TEST ROUTES

A list of the test routes, operated by the IAM at the time of going to press, is given below. You can take the advanced test anywhere you like in the UK; a route is always available near your home address. If you are in any doubt, the IAM will confirm which current route is most convenient for you.

Aberdeen
Aylesbury
Ayr
Banff
Bangor
Barnsley
Bedford
Belfast
Berwick-on-Tweed
Birkenhead
Birmingham
Blackpool
Bodmin
Bolton
Boston
Bournemouth
Bradford
Bridgend
Brighton
Bristol
Bude
Burton-on-Trent
Bury St Edmunds
Cambridge

Canterbury
Cardiff
Carlisle
Chelmsford
Cheltenham
Chester
Chichester
Chorley
Colwyn Bay
Coventry
Crawley
Crewe
Darlington
Debenham
Derby
Dorchester
Dumfries
Dundee
Dunoon
Edinburgh
Elgin
Exeter
Folkestone
Galashiels

Glasgow
Grantham
Greenock
Grimsby
Guildford
Harrogate
Hartlepool
Haverfordwest
Hereford
Huddersfield
Hull
Huntly
Inverness
Ipswich
Isle of Man
Isle of Wight
Kendal
Kettering
Ladybank
Leeds
Leicester
Lichfield
Lincoln
Liverpool

Londonderry
Luton
Maidstone
Manchester
Mansfield
Middlesborough
Newark
Newcastle
Newmarket
Newport
Northampton
Norwich
Nottingham
Oban
Okehampton
Oxford
Penrith
Perth
Peterborough
Plymouth
Porthmadog
Portsmouth
Preston
Reading
Retford
Ripon
Rotherham
Scarborough

Scunthorpe
Sheffield
Shrewsbury
Southampton
Southend
St Austell
St Helens
Staines
Stockport
Stoke-on-Trent
Stowmarket
Sunderland
Swansea
Swindon
Taunton
Truro
Tunbridge Wells
Wakefield
Walsall
Watford
Wetherby
Wick
Widnes
Wigan
Winchester
Windsor
Woking
Wolverhampton

Worcester
Worksop
Worthing
Yeovil
York

London
Barnes
Crystal Palace
Harrow
Wanstead

West Germany
*(HM Forces and
British nationals on*
Bielefeld
Gutersloh
Hanover
Paderborn
Rheindahlen
Sennelager

Cyprus
*(HM Forces and
British nationals on*
Akrotiri
Larnaca

SIGNS AND SIGNALS

Traffic signs SIGNS GIVING ORDERS

These signs are mostly circular and those with red circles are mostly prohibitive

Maximum speed

National speed limit applies

Stop and Give Way

Give way to traffic on major road

School crossing patrol

No vehicles

No entry for vehicular traffic

No right turn

No left turn

No U turns

No overtaking

Give priority to vehicles from opposite direction

No motor vehicles

No motor vehicles except solo motorcycles, scooters or mopeds

Manually operated temporary 'STOP' sign

No vehicles with over 12 seats except regular scheduled, school and works buses

No cycling

No pedestrians

No goods vehicles over maximum gross weight shown (in tonnes)

No vehicles including load over weight shown (in tonnes)

Axle weight limit in tonnes

No vehicles over height shown

No vehicle or combination of vehicles over length shown

.No vehicles over width shown

No stopping (Clearway)

Permit holders **only**
Parking restricted to use by people named on sign

URBAN CLEARWAY Monday to Friday
am 8·9 30 pm 4 30 6 30
No stopping during times shown except for as long as necessary to set down or pick up passengers

Plates below some signs qualify their message

End	Except for loading	Except buses and coaches	Except buses	Except for access
End of restriction	Exception for loading/unloading goods	Exception for vehicles with over 12 seats	Exception for stage and scheduled express carriages, school and works buses	Exception for access to premises and land adjacent to the road where there is no alternative route

Signs with blue circles but no red border mostly give positive instruction

Ahead only

Turn left ahead (right if symbol reversed)

Turn left (right if symbol reversed)

Keep left (right if symbol reversed)

Vehicles may pass either side to reach same destination

Route to be used by pedal cycles only

Minimum speed

End of minimum speed

Mini-roundabout (roundabout circulation – give way to vehicles from the immediate right)

One-way traffic
(Note: compare circular "Ahead only" sign)

Shared pedal cycle and pedestrian route

With-flow bus and cycle lane

Contra-flow bus lane

With-flow pedal cycle lane

WARNING SIGNS *Mostly triangular*

STOP
100 yds

Distance to
"STOP"
line ahead

Cross roads

Roundabout

T junction

Staggered junction

GIVE WAY
50 yds

Distance to
"Give Way"
line ahead

Double bend
first to left
(may be reversed)

REDUCE
SPEED
NOW

Plate below
some signs

◀◀◀◀
Sharp deviation
of route to left
(or right if
chevrons reversed)

Bend to right
(or left if symbol reversed)

Dual carriageway
ends

Slippery road

Two-way traffic
straight ahead

Two-way traffic
crosses
one-way road

Traffic merges from left/right
with equal priority

Road narrows on
right (left if
symbol reversed)

Road narrows
on both sides

**Elderly
people**

Crossing point
for elderly
people (blind or
disabled if shown)

No footway
for 400 yds

Pedestrians in
road ahead

Pedestrian
crossing

School

Children going to
or from school

Patrol

School crossing
patrol ahead
(Some signs have
amber lights which
flash when
patrol is operating)

Uneven road

Traffic
signals

Failure of
light signals

10%
Steep hill
downwards

20%
Steep hill
upwards

Gradients may be shown as a ratio
i.e. 20% = 1:5

Risk of Grounding

Risk of grounding
of long low
vehicles at
level crossing

Road works

Hump bridge

Change to opposite
carriageway
(may be reversed)

Loose
chippings

Ford

Worded warning
sign

AUTOMATIC
BARRIERS
STOP
when
lights show

Plate to indicate
a level crossing
equipped with
automatic barriers
and flashing lights

Level crossing
with barrier
or gate ahead

Level crossing
without barrier
or gate ahead

Level crossing
without barrier
(the additional
lower half of the cross
is used when there
is more than one
railway line)

Cycle route ahead

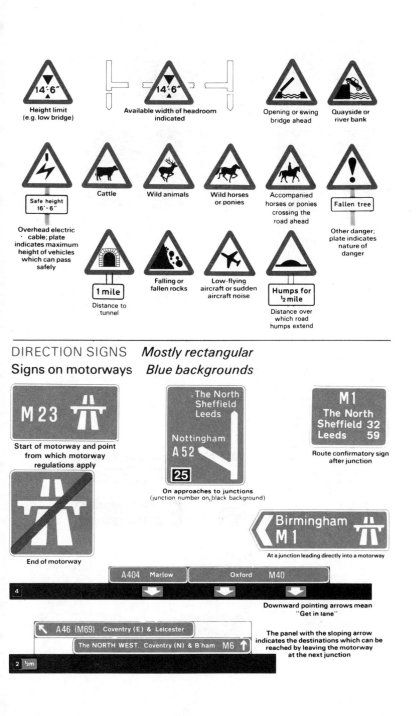

Height limit
(e.g. low bridge)

Available width of headroom
indicated

Opening or swing
bridge ahead

Quayside or
river bank

Cattle

Wild animals

Wild horses
or ponies

Accompanied
horses or ponies
crossing the
road ahead

Overhead electric
cable; plate
indicates maximum
height of vehicles
which can pass
safely

Other danger;
plate indicates
nature of
danger

Distance to
tunnel

Falling or
fallen rocks

Low-flying
aircraft or sudden
aircraft noise

Distance over
which road
humps extend

DIRECTION SIGNS   *Mostly rectangular*
Signs on motorways *Blue backgrounds*

Start of motorway and point
from which motorway
regulations apply

On approaches to junctions
(junction number on black background)

Route confirmatory sign
after junction

End of motorway

At a junction leading directly into a motorway

Downward pointing arrows mean
"Get in lane"

The panel with the sloping arrow
indicates the destinations which can be
reached by leaving the motorway
at the next junction

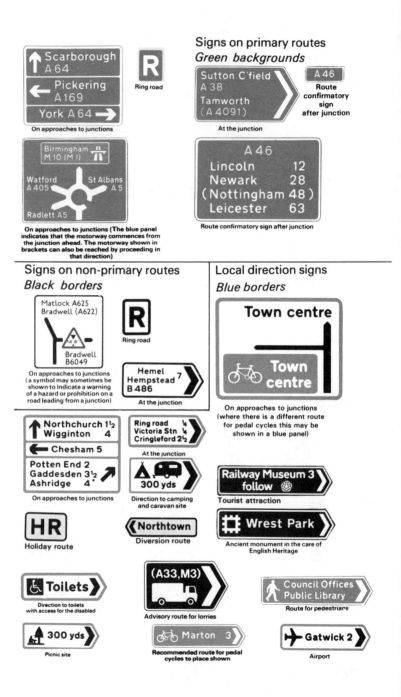

Signs on primary routes
Green backgrounds

Scarborough A 64

Pickering A 169

York A 64

R — Ring road

On approaches to junctions

Sutton C'field A 38 / Tamworth (A 4091)

At the junction

A 46 — Route confirmatory sign after junction

Birmingham M 10 (M 1) / Watford A 405 / St Albans A 5 / Radlett A5

On approaches to junctions (The blue panel indicates that the motorway commences from the junction ahead. The motorway shown in brackets can also be reached by proceeding in that direction)

A 46
Lincoln 12
Newark 28
(Nottingham 48)
Leicester 63

Route confirmatory sign after junction

Signs on non-primary routes
Black borders

Matlock A625
Bradwell (A622)
14'6"
Bradwell B6049

On approaches to junctions (a symbol may sometimes be shown to indicate a warning of a hazard or prohibition on a road leading from a junction)

R — Ring road

Hemel Hempstead 7 B 486 — At the junction

Northchurch 1½
Wigginton 4
Chesham 5
Potten End 2
Gaddesden 3½
Ashridge 4

On approaches to junctions

Ring road ¼
Victoria Stn ¼
Cringleford 2½

At the junction

300 yds — Direction to camping and caravan site

HR — Holiday route

Northtown — Diversion route

Toilets — Direction to toilets with access for the disabled

(A33,M3) — Advisory route for lorries

300 yds — Picnic site

Marton 3 — Recommended route for pedal cycles to place shown

Local direction signs
Blue borders

Town centre

Town centre

On approaches to junctions (where there is a different route for pedal cycles this may be shown in a blue panel)

Railway Museum 3 follow — Tourist attraction

Wrest Park — Ancient monument in the care of English Heritage

Council Offices Public Library — Route for pedestrians

Gatwick 2 — Airport

INFORMATION SIGNS   *All rectangular*

Meter **ZONE**

Mon-Fri
8·30 am-6·30 pm
Saturday
8·30 am-1·30 pm

**Entrance to
controlled
parking zone**

One-way street

**Parking place for
towed caravans**

**Priority over vehicles
from opposite
direction**

Weight limit
10 tonnes
3 miles
ahead

**Advance warning of
restriction or prohibition
ahead**

**No through
road**

Hospital

**Hospital
ahead**

Forton
Services ¹2m

Petrol **::**   *180.5* p

**Distance to service area with fuel,
parking and cafeteria facilities
(The current petrol price may be shown
in pence per gallon or litre,
or may be omitted)**

Zone
ENDS

**End of
controlled
parking zone**

**Appropriate traffic lanes
at junction ahead**

**"Count-down" markers at exit from motorway
(each bar represents 100 yards to the exit).
Green-backed markers may be used on primary
routes and white-backed markers with red bars
on the approaches to concealed level crossings**

**Recommended route
for pedal cycles**

Tourist
information
**Tourist
information
point**

**Permanent
reduction in
available lanes,
e.g. two-lane
carriageway
reducing to one**

Temporary lane closure

The number and position of arrows and red
bars may be varied according to lanes open
and closed

Bus lane

**Bus lane on road
at junction ahead**

Lane control signals

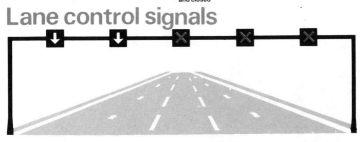

White arrow — lane available to traffic facing the sign. Red crosses — lane closed to traffic facing the sign.

Light signals controlling traffic

TRAFFIC LIGHT SIGNALS

   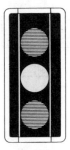

RED means "Stop". Wait behind the stop line on the carriageway.

RED AND AMBER also means "Stop". Do not pass through or start until GREEN shows.

GREEN means you may go on if the way is clear. Take special care if you mean to turn left or right and give way to pedestrians who are crossing.

AMBER means "Stop" at the stop line. You may go on only if the AMBER appears after you have crossed the stop line or are so close to it that to pull up might cause an accident.

A GREEN ARROW may be provided in addition to the full green signal if movement in a certain direction is allowed before or after the full green phase. If the way is clear you may go but only in the direction shown by the arrow. You may do this whatever other lights may be showing.

FLASHING RED LIGHTS

Alternately flashing red lights mean YOU MUST STOP

At level crossings, lifting bridges, airfields, fire stations, etc

Road markings
ACROSS THE CARRIAGEWAY

Give way to traffic on major road

Give way to traffic from the right in roundabout

Give way to traffic from right at mini-roundabout

Stop line at "STOP" sign

Stop line at signals or police control

ALONG THE CARRIAGEWAY

Double white lines

See Rules 71 and 72

Diagonal stripes

See Rule 73

Lane markings

Lane line
See Rules 74 and 75

Centre line

Hazard warning line
See Rule 70

ALONG THE EDGE OF THE CARRIAGEWAY
Waiting restrictions

No waiting on carriageway, pavement or verge (except to load or unload or while passengers board or alight) at times shown on nearby plates or on entry signs to controlled parking zones.

If no days are indicated on the sign, the restrictions are in force every day including Sundays and Bank Holidays. The lines give a guide to the restriction in force but the time plates must be consulted.

Examples of plates indicating restriction times

Continuous prohibition

Plate giving times

Limited waiting

| No waiting for at least eight hours between 7 am and 7 pm on four or more days of the week | No waiting for at least eight hours between 7 am and 7 pm on four or more days of the week plus some additional period outside these times | During any other periods |

ON THE KERB OR AT THE EDGE OF THE CARRIAGEWAY
Loading restrictions

No loading or unloading at times shown on nearby plates. If no days are indicated on the sign, the restrictions are in force every day including Sundays and Bank Holidays.

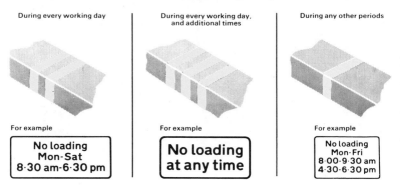

During every working day	During every working day, and additional times	During any other periods
For example	For example	For example
No loading Mon-Sat 8·30 am-6·30 pm	No loading at any time	No loading Mon-Fri 8·00-9·30 am 4·30-6·30 pm

ZEBRA CONTROLLED AREAS

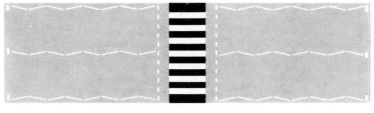

OTHER ROAD MARKINGS

Keep entrance clear of stationary vehicles, even if picking up or setting down children

Warning of "Give Way" **just ahead**	**Parking space reserved** **for vehicles named**	**See Rule 124**	**See Rule 82**

Box junction
 See Rule 99 | **Do not block entrance**
 to side road | **Indication of traffic lanes**

Note: Although *The Highway Code* shows many of the signs
commonly in use, a comprehensive explanation of our signing system
is given in the Department's booklet *Know Your Traffic Signs*, which
is on sale at booksellers. The booklet also illustrates and explains the
vast majority of signs the road user is likely to encounter.
The signs illustrated in *The Highway Code* are not all drawn to the
same scale. In Wales, bilingual versions of some signs are used.